ARAGON
ISSUES IN
PHILOSOPHY

PARAGON ISSUES IN PHILOSOPHY

THE PARAGON ISSUES IN PHILOSOPHY SERIES

At colleges and universities, interest in the traditional areas of philosophy remains strong. Many new currents flow within them, too, but some of these—the rise of cognitive science, for example, or feminist philosophy—went largely unnoticed in undergraduate philosophy courses until the end of the 1980s. The Paragon Issues in Philosophy Series responds to both perennial and newly influential concerns by bringing together a team of able philosophers to address the fundamental issues in philosophy today and to outline the state of contemporary discussion about them.

More than twenty volumes are scheduled; they are organized into three major categories. The first covers the standard topics—metaphysics, theory of knowledge, ethics, and political philosophy—stressing innovative developments in those disciplines. The second focuses on more specialized but still vital concerns in the philosophies of science, religion, history, sport, and other areas. The third category explores new work that relates philosophy and fields such as feminist criticism, medicine, economics, technology, and literature.

The level of writing is aimed at undergraduate students who have little previous experience studying philosophy. The books provide brief but accurate introductions that appraise the state of the art in their fields and show how the history of thought about their topics developed. Each volume is complete in itself but also complements others in the series.

Traumatic change characterizes these last years of the twentieth century: all of it involves philosophical issues. The editorial staff at Paragon House has worked with us to develop this series. We hope it will encourage the understanding needed in our times, which are as complicated and problematic as they are promising.

John K. Roth
Claremont McKenna College

Frederick Sontag
Pomona College

SOCIAL
AND
POLITICAL
PHILOSOPHY

WILLIAM L. McBRIDE

SOCIAL AND POLITICAL PHILOSOPHY

PARAGON
ISSUES IN
PHILOSOPHY

PARAGON HOUSE • NEW YORK

FIRST EDITION, 1994

PUBLISHED IN THE UNITED STATES BY

PARAGON HOUSE
370 LEXINGTON AVENUE
NEW YORK, NEW YORK 10017

COPYRIGHT © 1994 BY WILLIAM L. McBRIDE

LIBRARY OF CONGRESS CATALOGING-IN-PUBLICATION DATA

McBRIDE, WILLIAM LEON.
    SOCIAL AND POLITICAL PHILOSOPHY / WILLIAM L. McBRIDE.—1ST ED.
    P.   CM.   —(PARAGON ISSUES IN PHILOSOPHY)
    INCLUDES BIBLIOGRAPHICAL REFERENCES AND INDEX.
    ISBN 1-55778-220-2
    1. SOCIAL   SCIENCES—PHILOSOPHY. 2. POLITICAL   SCIENCE—
PHILOSOPHY.
    I. TITLE.   II. SERIES.
    H61.M38   1993
    300'.1—DC20   92-44094
                                                        CIP

MANUFACTURED IN THE UNITED STATES OF AMERICA

CONTENTS

INTRODUCTION

I t was the ancient Greek philosopher Aristotle who first made explicit the rationale for social and political philosophy. "The human being," he said, "is by nature a political animal." And since one way of characterizing the enterprise of philosophy is as a systematic effort to understand the underlying principles of all sorts of things, it is natural that the investigation of *political* things should constitute an important part of the total philosophic enterprise.

In philosophy, seemingly simple assertions such as this one of Aristotle's are often fraught with complex implications. For example, when Aristotle refers to what something is "by nature" he is relying on a whole web of assumptions about the equivalence of what is "natural" with what is right and good. Some later philosophers would challenge these assumptions as being either wrong or at least unsubstantiated. Moreover, the Greek adjective *politikon*, which I have translated straightforwardly as "political," is based on the noun for the Greek city-state, the *polis*. Philosophers and ordinary citizens alike saw the *polis* as more all-encompassing for their lives than any institution that we would call political is for us nowadays. The *polis* was the milieu of Greek civil society as well as of government. So it is perhaps more accurate to translate Aristotle as saying that the human being is by nature a social and political animal.

As Aristotle himself knew well, political institutions in the narrower sense—kingships, democratic parliaments, supreme councils made up of members of aristocratic ruling elites, or whatever—are fully understandable only in terms of other institutions and practices of the particular societies in which they are located. Thus it makes better sense today to designate the subject matter of this book as "social and political philosophy" rather than the more traditional "political philosophy," since the latter *might* be taken to imply an exclusive emphasis on principles of government. One could, of course, try to divide up the two subject matters, the social and the political elements, analogously to the way in which sociology and political science are generally considered two separate disciplines in American colleges and universities today. But to do this in philosophy seems unnecessarily artificial. This is because of the actual interconnection of the two domains at the deep level with which philosophy is concerned and because most of the best-known philosophers in the Western tradition, from Plato and Aristotle to Hegel, Marx, Mill, and beyond, have in fact written about broader social issues as well as political institutions.

If Aristotle's conception of the compass of "politics" was in an important sense a broad one, in another sense it was narrower than I consider acceptable for the purposes of this book. The geographic scope of the *polis*, the city-state, was, as its name suggests, very limited. Aristotle explicitly says that any "political" territory that cannot readily be surveyed and from which not all citizens have easy egress is inordinately large. True, there was a significant philosophical movement, Stoicism, in ancient times subsequent to Aristotle's that proposed a vision of a universal political order, the "cosmopolis." Stoicism thus broke completely with Aristotle in this respect. But the Stoic vision was quite abstract and general, reliant in large measure on metaphysical intuitions about the nature of the world rather than on specific societal or political facts. Incorporated in various versions into the new worldview of Christianity, the idea of the cosmopolis continued to exert influence over medieval political thought, but it fell into comparative oblivion with the rise of the modern nation-state. It was the latter that, as we shall see, replaced Aristotle's city-state as the focal unit of early modern social and political philosophy.

It is my conviction that this focus is becoming outmoded today and hence that a contemporary textbook in social and political philosophy must take into account the *global* dimensions of its topics, even though most of the published literature even today still presupposes that the nation-state is the principal political unit.

What is the relationship between social/political philosophy, or theory, and actual practice? From the standpoint of chronological priority, the answer is obvious: There were social structures and political institutions long before human beings began systematically to reflect upon or philosophize about them. But to acknowledge this is not equivalent to saying that social and political philosophies are nothing but passive reflections, or mirror images, of the societies in which they are written. To the extent to which philosophies were indeed like this, and to the extent to which they were to justify or legitimize the existing sociopolitical orders as the best possible, they would amount to mere ideologies, a term first brought into vogue by Marx. However, it can easily be documented that the worthwhile social and political philosophies always contain an active, creative aspect, one that takes some distance from the present state of affairs and that, by doing so, also implies some *criticism* of this present state.

Marx's famous dictum about this question of theory and practice was that the philosophers had interpreted the world in various ways, whereas the point was to change it. But Marx's own work was fundamentally philosophical in nature. His is another interpretation of the sociopolitical world—one that, like those before and since, claims to be in some way superior in insight to the rest. At the same time, it *did* change the world in many ways, not all of which would have been to Marx's liking. This is inevitable. However clear the philosopher's insight may have been, however definite his or her critical vision of how the sociopolitical world ought to be by comparison with the way it is, any attempt to implement or put into practice some of these ideas is certain to involve distortions of the original philosophy. There are many good reasons for this. A philosophy, once written (or taught orally) by an individual, must fall into others' hands if it is to have any effect. Those others are just that: *other*, each with a somewhat different total perspective on the world.

In treating our subject, I have thought it best to begin by surveying some of the great moments and ideas in the history of Western social and political philosophy; this survey will constitute Chapters 1 through 4. It is essential to note, especially in view of the previous remarks about the need today to adopt a global vision beyond the nation-state model, that it is *Western* thought (in the broad, conventional sense of the term: Europe and the heirs of the European colonists), rather than Asian, African, or Native American, upon which I draw primarily for this historical survey. This choice is not meant as a judgment concerning which ideas, individuals, or cultures are intrinsically most valuable, in accordance with some supposedly universal standards. Such standards may not exist. But, for better or worse, past Western social and political philosophies have had an enormous, cumulative effect on today's "One World," and this implies a need to study them here.

There is also an element of choice involved in trying to stake out the territory of our subject matter. This involves more than just determining that strictly political issues are ultimately inseparable from broader questions about the nature of society. There are other domains of philosophy that seem closely related to the one that we are entering. Ethics, philosophy of law, and ontology or metaphysics (what Aristotle called "first philosophy") are three that come to mind. Although many philosophers have given good systematic reasons for insisting on one or another scheme of division, none is unproblematic and all are subject to philosophical questioning. Aristotle, for instance, saw ethics as subsumable under social and political philosophy, since he regarded habituation, training from early childhood, to ethical behavior as being feasible only in a properly ordered community. But thinkers with anarchist tendencies regard political institutions as *barriers* to the realization of a fully ethical life.

Law has many distinctive qualities not characteristic of other social and political institutions, but it is nevertheless one such institution. Moreover, the philosophy of law must inevitably deal with certain concepts, such as justice and rights, with which social and political philosophy also deals. Similarly, as far as ontology or metaphysics is concerned, no systematic thinking about society and politics really takes place in total absence of ontological presuppositions about the ultimate reality of which the sociopolitical world is a part.

Another philosophical field of study closely interconnected with social and political philosophy, as well as with ethics, the philosophy of law, ontology, and other areas, is feminist thought, the topic of another monograph in the series of which this book is a part. The absence of all but a few, mostly demeaning, references to women in traditional social/political philosophy helps to explain the current need for philosophies of women, but it is also unquestionably a serious problem *in* and *for* social and political philosophy. Some of the influence of recent feminist writing will become evident in later chapters.

A contemporary French thinker, Gilles Deleuze, has proposed substituting the metaphor of the *rhizome* for more traditional metaphors about "roots" and "branches" of philosophy. Plants that grow rhizomatically, of which crabgrass is a common example, tend to lack clear, symmetrical structures such as one finds in classic stately trees. There is a certain wildness, a certain unpredictability, about rhizomatic growth. This metaphor, too, can be abused and overemphasized, but it is a useful corrective to our natural wish to be able to effect clear-cut divisions within philosophy or even between philosophy and other disciplines, so that we can "know" exactly where social and political philosophy begins and leaves off.

Thus, the divisions of this textbook subsequent to the historical survey chapters will have a certain systematic, schematic basis, but it would be a misapprehension to regard that schema as anything more than one among several plausible possibilities. The schema that I employ runs roughly as follows. Among the philosophical topics that today seem to be most widely mentioned, discussed, and debated around the world are the related notions of freedom and rights. They have both social and political (as well as ontological, ethical, legal, etc.) dimensions. They are the background to talk of democracy in China, the former Soviet Union, and virtually everywhere else, as well as of "hot" issues from abortion to drug and gun control to corporate responsibility toward the environment in the United States. They also lie, for example, behind allusions to the possibility of canceling crushing debt-payment burdens, in the face of bank credi-tors' property-rights claims, in the Third World. Rights and freedom are the subject matter of Chapter 5.

But a full understanding of competing rights claims becomes possible only in light of the broader question, deemed central to the first great classic of Western social and political philosophy, Plato's *Republic*, about the nature of justice. This topic, which underwent a great revival in popularity among philosophers during the 1970s and is still very much front and center, is the focus of Chapter 6. However, the notion of "justice," like that of "rights," can be very abstract. Demands for rights and justice usually originate in concrete human situations where it is felt that they are not being honored. What seems to be presupposed by such demands is some notion of ideal human community. Plato saw this very clearly: his abstract definition of justice as everyone's performing his or her own proper task comes to life and makes sense only in the context of the concrete picture of what we would now call a "utopian" society that he sketches. Chapter 7 thus focuses on such ideals, without, of course, presupposing agreement with Plato's or any other writer's utopian conception, but also without presupposing the negative bias implicit for some in the word *utopia*. Such "ideal community" notions will lead me to rein-troduce the "One World" theme already mentioned. This is consid-ered in a final chapter as a guide to suggestions about some possible future directions for social and political philosophizing.

Within this schematic framework, my purpose is to try to convey salient topics, arguments, and viewpoints without unduly emphasiz-ing those I prefer. For example, I consider much current talk about both rights and justice misguided and confused. I believe it to be an illusion, promoted by Plato on the basis of his conception of the nature of knowledge and reality, that something called perfect justice is knowable and definable. But I shall not belabor my own arguments in support of these convictions at the expense of other viewpoints. In fact, although I have no doubt that rigorous argumentation is an essential *component* of philosophy, my approach throughout is itself generally more narrative than argumentative. This happens to be in keeping with some increasingly popular contemporary views about the nature of the philosophic enterprise, although my reasons for favoring this approach do not depend on its affinity with these trends. Rather, it simply seems to me to be the best way of acquainting students with the broad scope of the subject matter of social and political philosophy from both historical and contemporary perspectives as well as with the suppressed but nevertheless real and strong passion that always lies beneath its surface. For, in the answers given to the questions that social/political philosophy raises, nothing less than the configuration of the communities in which we must live is at stake.

A BRIEF HISTORY: ANCIENT BEGINNINGS

dentifiably philosophical thinking in Western culture cannot be said to have begun on a set date and in a set place. Rather, what written records we retain suggest that the gradual evolution of efforts systematically and critically to explain the world grew out of less systematic religious stories and prescientific folk wisdom. A standard convention of historians of thought designates Thales, a widely reputed "Wise Man" of an early period in Greek civilization (early sixth century B.C.), as the first philosopher. Fragmentary recorded sayings of his attempt to offer unified explanations of a universal sort—namely, that all things are made of water and are full of the gods. We have no record of Thales' sociopolitical views. In general the so-called Pre-Socratics, a blanket term for a large number of early philosophical thinkers in Greece and Greek outposts around the Mediterranean, concentrated above all on giving accounts of the physical, natural world. However, a few of their contributions are of special interest for us, as are some contributions by literary figures and historians.

Anaximander (mid-sixth century B.C.), for example, in an extant fragment, stresses the role of a sort of cosmic *justice*. This is seen as a balancing of accounts in preserving an ultimate harmony in the universe. (In metaphorical dress, this idea is still embodied in the statues of the blindfolded woman with the scales so familiar in Western courthouse architecture.) As he says, existing things "give justice and make reparation to one another for injustice according to the order of time." Heraclitus (late sixth and early fifth century B.C.), known as "the Obscure" for his allusive, epigrammatic style, stressed the eternal changeableness of everything, the fact that nothing ever remains the same, as well as the preeminent role of conflict or strife in the world. He himself appears to have had a very aristocratic worldview, stressing differences in worth among human beings and spurning egalitarianism. However, his insight into the universality of change and conflict between opposing forces inspired Marx's colleague Friedrich Engels, a strong egalitarian, to single out Heraclitus as the first great proponent of the dialectical method that is of such central importance to the Marxist account of the possibility of revolution. In fact, this strange, paradoxical instance of important common ground between thinkers with radically opposed sociopolitical outlooks in other areas is only the first of many we shall encounter. The history of social and political philosophy is filled with stories of simultaneous attractions and repulsions among its principal figures.

More or less contemporary with Heraclitus, and deeply at odds with his love of change and conflict, was Parmenides, to whom Plato later devoted one of his dialogues. His insistence that "The Way of Truth," the title of one of his twin philosophical poems, entailed rejecting "The Way of Opinion [*doxa*]," the title of the other, and clinging to the pure oneness and immutability of Being has no *immediate* implications for social and political theory. Nevertheless the work of Parmenides serves beautifully to define the fundamental tension running throughout the entire history of Western philosophy, including its sociopolitical aspects. On the one hand, there is the feeling that the world "of opinion" as we experience it every day is confusing and often contradictory, hence difficult if not impossible to understand or explain. Yet, by articulating and *describing* its confusions and contradictoriness, thus "saving the appearances" (to use a slogan of some of the ancient Greeks), we are in fact beginning to explain it in a unifying fashion.

On the other hand, there is a deep longing for the sort of pure, unencumbered, radiant, and total overview of the world of society and politics for which most logic and mathematics provide the obvious model. This tempts thinkers to create images of an ideal, perfect state—a city of dreams, bathed in an unworldly light and perhaps set on a hill —but as soon as we proceed to imagine its concrete details, much less try to implement a few of them in the world in which we live, we are confronted once again with the need to deal with messy appearances and with so-called "commonsense" opinions.

Political themes, of course, were prominent in the nonphilosophical literature of Ancient Greece. The epics of Homer, whose preeminent status within that culture disturbed Plato greatly because of their frequent depiction of so-called heroes and even of gods engaging in what could only be considered deeply immoral activity (gross deceit, outright murder), essentially concern a series of political events: the war of conquest against Troy by an alliance of Greek city-states and its aftermath. Hesiod's less heroic classic, *Works and Days*, portrays interesting aspects of the social lives of ordinary people. But by roughly the middle of the fifth century B.C., the time now seen as Greece's Golden Age, literature was beginning to go beyond the mere depiction of social and political themes to the presentation of recognizably philosophical issues about politics and society.

An example of this is the drama of the great playwright Sophocles entitled *Antigone*. An already classic story is recounted in such a way as to bring out both the intellectual and the practical dimensions of Antigone's dilemma. That dilemma involved whether to abide by the decree of her uncle Creon, king of Thebes, not to bury the body of her slain rebel brother Polyneices or to flout it by observing the burial rituals for aiding family members' passage to the Underworld that were considered by her culture to be the gods' unwritten and unfailing laws. "Not now, nor yesterday's, they always live, and no one knows their origin in time."[1] Antigone does not hesitate to follow the divine law, as she understands it, against the human law and to pay the penalty. The play is replete with arguments, involving the Chorus and the principal characters, concerning the justifiability or unjustifiability of civil disobedience, the relative weights of the laws of the upper and nether worlds, and even the feminist issue of whether Antigone's heroic stance should be discounted by virtue of her sex. In the early nineteenth century Hegel was to regard the Antigone story as a dramatization of the early Greek world's important transition from a tribal to a more recognizably political culture. This transition had of course been completed by Sophocles' time.

The Biblical book of Job is another literary classic, equally pervaded with religious elements, that dates from approximately the same time and comes from a different culture that shares with ancient Greece the role of shaping Western philosophy. It too has important sociopolitical implications. As an account of the monumental sufferings of a legendary figure in the earlier history of the Middle East, it serves as a vehicle for questioning the conventional wisdom represented by Job's ironically named "comforters." This was that earthly misfortune was a sign of God's displeasure with the sufferer; hence, cosmic justice really does prevail in the everyday world.

In the process of arguing that he has in fact been a God-fearing, pious person, Job expresses a wish that he might plead his case before God as in a law court, since he is confident that he would then be vindicated. The "resolution" of the debate, such as it is, comes in the form of God's speaking from a desert storm and stressing His own incomprehensibly great power. This is shown by such earthly creations of His as the Leviathan, an enormous animal, to which "nothing upon the earth can be compared." This notion of an earthly representation of God was to be used by Thomas Hobbes centuries later as the central metaphor for the unlimited political sovereignty that he advocates in his sociopolitical classic *Leviathan*.

Within less than forty years of the date (441 B.C.) *Antigone* was first produced, the face of the Greek world had been completely altered by the series of events known as the Peloponnesian War, an episode of profound importance for the whole subsequent history of Western social and political thought. A united Greek force had repulsed the invading Persian armies early in the century. This created a situation that made possible an imperial hegemony for Athens, leader of the victorious Greek city-states. Many smaller city-states were expected to pay tribute for protection to an Athens-dominated alliance. This wealth, combined with Athens' preeminence as a trading center for the whole eastern Mediterranean world, enabled its political leadership to construct many of the great monuments and in general to support the outpouring of artistic development, the fruits of which we still enjoy.

Sparta, a powerful, landlocked city-state located farther south, in the Peloponnesian Peninsula, deeply resented Athenian hegemony and began militarily to challenge it and to create a counterleague of its own. Fortunately, we have a detailed analysis and description of the background and the first twenty years of this war from the stylus of an Athenian exile, Thucydides. Often considered the first modern (critical, reflective, as opposed to merely chronicling) work of history, it is at the same time a very significant landmark in the historical development of social and political philosophy.

Outstanding among the features of Thucydides' history is the oration he imputes to the principal Athenian political leader of the time, Pericles, on the occasion of the public burial of the first Athenian casualties of the war. Pericles, an acquaintance of Plato's father and soon to die himself, pronounces a beautiful tribute to the Athenian way of life, by contrast with the Spartan, as seen by one of its principal proponents and beneficiaries. Of course, it is an idealization: All was not well even at this point, as Athenian imperialism had in fact contributed to sowing the seeds of the war. Athenian society was ostensibly democratic, but only for the 10 percent or so of the overall population who were adult male citizens and not women, slaves, children, or resident aliens. It was in fact guided in its major policy decisions by the ruling elite of which Pericles was primus inter pares, the first among equals. Nevertheless, Pericles' words are inspiring, as can be sensed from this excerpt:

Our constitution does not copy the laws of neighboring states; we are rather a pattern to others than imitators ourselves. Its administration favors the many instead of the few; this is why it is called a democracy. If we look to the laws, they afford equal justice to all in their private differences; if to social standing, advancement in public life falls to reputation for capacity, class considerations not being allowed to interfere with merit; nor again does poverty bar the way. . . . The freedom which we enjoy in our government extends also to our ordinary life. . . .[2]

Readers who have not already done so are urged to absorb the whole text of this speech.

Soon thereafter, as Thucydides recounts, there occurred a severe and ravaging plague that killed a large number of Athenians. A great change, he says, took place in citizens' outlooks and behaviors. The old burial rites, once considered so sacred, were ignored; people began to look only to momentary pleasure and to disregard all the values once held in highest esteem, such as personal honor, and in short "Fear of gods or law of man there was none to restrain them."[3] This historical "transvaluation of values" was later attributed by many Athenians as much to the flourishing of the group of itinerant teachers and freethinkers known as the Sophists ("wise guys," as distinguished from "wise men," is a suggestive rough translation) as to the plague and other calamities that befell Athens. As we shall see, it was this condition of sociocultural malaise against which Plato was to attempt to crusade in his brilliant dialogues, while contending that Socrates had not been just another Sophist. This same notion of transvaluation of values, now regarded as eminently *desirable* in the context of an allegedly decadent late nineteenth-century European culture, was to be taken up and advocated by Friedrich Nietzsche.

One more episode in Thucydides' history merits special attention in a survey of the history of social and political philosophy. This is the conference held, in the sixteenth year of the war, on the small island of Melos between its leaders and some envoys from Athens. A Spartan colony, Melos wished to remain neutral in the war, something the Athenians considered unacceptable. The words Thucydides puts in their mouths (he was not actually there, but attempted, as was his custom, to reconstruct what was said from the information he had) are as chilling an expression of pure raison d'etat—the assertion of naked power against a powerless people—as one can find in all of literature.

The Athenians begin by saying that they will dispense with specious rhetoric about their own supposed claims to loyalty from other city-states as a result of their role in the war against the Persians. They then define the "mutual advantage" involved in their proposal of submission to be that the Melians will avoid a worse fate by submitting, while at the same time the Athenians will save themselves the trouble of destroying them. Finally, they reject the Melians' appeals to standards of virtue and to the gods:

When you speak of the favor of the gods, we may as fairly hope for that as yourselves. . . . Of the gods we believe, and of men we know, that by a necessary law of nature they rule wherever they can. And it is not as if we were the first to make this law, or to act upon it when made: we found it existing before us, and shall leave it to exist forever after us; all we do is to make use of it, knowing that you and everybody else, having the same power as we have, would do the same as we do.[4]

The Melians refused the offer and were duly besieged by Athenian forces. "Some treachery taking place inside," Thucydides cryptically concludes his chapter, "the Melians surrendered at discretion to the Athenians, who put to death all the grown men whom they took, and sold the women and children for slaves, and subsequently sent out five hundred colonists and inhabited the place themselves."[5]

The spirit of Melos—naked power, naked self-interest—is precisely the central challenge that Plato poses in the opening section of his *Republic*. It is not that he mentions by name the Melian episode or indeed any specific episode of the Peloponnesian War; he did not need to do so for his reading audience. By the time he wrote, the war was a matter of past history. Athens had lost and, through a sequence of events indirectly resulting from this loss, his teacher Socrates had been tried and executed. But he uses the figure of Thrasymachus of Chalcedon, an actual Sophist who taught and wrote extensively on rhetoric, as a vehicle to express the spirit of Melos by maintaining that justice is nothing but the interest of the stronger.

In short, to use a more modern formulation, Thrasymachus is claiming, as did the Athenian envoys at the Melian conference, that "might makes right." Socrates, Plato's spokesperson and central figure here as in almost all of his written dialogues, very quickly demolishes Thrasymachus' stated position by showing its inherent vagueness and, once elaborated upon, its incoherence. (For example, he easily shows that what the strong ruler *thinks* may be in his interest and what, in one of several more ultimate senses, will prove to have been in his best interest may be radically different.) But Glaucon and Adeimantus, two characters in the dialogue and in real life Plato's older brothers, are then depicted as posing a much more formidable challenge for Socrates than did Thrasymachus' facile dictum. They recount the story of a mythical shepherd named Gyges who found a magical ring that would make him invisible whenever he wished, thus enabling him quickly to "rise to the top" by a series of vicious acts for which he knew he would suffer no sanction. They then ask whether any human being if confronted with similar possibilities would in fact behave according to conventional notions of justice and honor.

Plato wrote two other dialogues in the area of social and political philosophy, the shorter *Statesman* (*Politicus*), which emphasizes the interrelationship between established laws and the craft of politics and, in its somewhat less bold and more moderate tone, anticipates elements of Aristotle's *Politics*, and *The Laws*, a lengthy product of Plato's old age that places somewhat more confidence in the existence of long-established institutional structures and in the guidance of elder statesmen. Nevertheless, the *Republic* is both his most provocative and his most influential dialogue, and so I shall confine myself to it for purposes of this survey. It is characteristic of Plato's subtle and complex style of thinking and writing that details of the physical setting of the dialogue are crucial for conveying many of his most important theoretical points.

The *Republic* begins with a vignette of Socrates, the supreme intellectual without political or business connections, who lives in the shadow of the Acropolis, Athens' majestic and sacred hill. He is en route back home (a walk of about seven miles) from a visit to the Piraeus, the bustling, confusing commercial port where strange phenomena from all over the known world were to be observed. A young friend, Polemarchus, sees him and invites him to come to Cephalus' (his father's) house to join in a friendly philosophical discussion. Socrates demurs, whereupon Polemarchus jokingly threatens to coerce him into coming, since there are more people accompanying him than Socrates. To Socrates' retort that he might be able to persuade them to let him go, Polemarchus responds that persuasion will not work on people unwilling to listen. They soon reach the house, where Socrates' first conversation is with Cephalus. He is presented as a virtuous, pious old man who possesses moderate wealth, less than his grandfather had accumulated but more than his father had left him. He has come to terms very well with the fact of being old. The advantage of such moderate wealth, he says by way of carrying on his conversation with Socrates, is that it obviates the temptation to be dishonest or to fail to repay one's debts.

But, Socrates asks, is being truthful and repaying debts identical with doing what is right or just? (In ancient Greek, a single word was used equally both for justice, which in modern English usage usually refers to a social or community context, and for righteousness or fairness on the part of an individual.) For example, he continues, should we always tell the strict truth to a madman, or return to such a person a weapon that we may once have borrowed from him in better times? Cephalus says that these are interesting questions but that he must now leave to perform a religious sacrifice and therefore will leave the discussion to his son and the others. This launches the debate on the nature of justice, into which Thrasymachus very soon interjects his radically amoral definition, and that debate continues for the remainder of the long dialogue.

In the space of a few paragraphs here at the beginning of the *Republic*, Plato has managed to introduce a number of the major questions that continue to this day to preoccupy social/political philosophers in the West. First, as we have already noted in drawing the parallel between the Athenian envoys at Melos and the position of Thrasymachus, does justice—assuming that we can reach some tentative consensus on what justice *means*—pay? Or, why be just? Should what conventional wisdom takes to be moral considerations predominate in the political order, or even in the ordering of (so to speak) our own individual souls? When, if ever, is coercion permissible? Is rhetorical persuasion itself not a kind of coercion? Can there be a purely logical, rational, nonrhetorical kind of persuasion? Is it possible to live a moral life without some wealth? If not, is it the obligation of the community as a whole, through its structures and political institutions, to make it possible for its citizens to enjoy wealth? If there is such an obligation, should wealth be made accessible to all or only to some? Should class divisions be permitted or even encouraged? Should *accumulation* of wealth by some individuals be allowed? If so, should any limit be placed on this? What is the purpose of a community as a whole? Should different individuals play different roles in it, and if so how should these differences be determined? What is the role of the intellectual? Should it be different from that of the ordinary citizen, and if so in what way? And so on.

Plato set the terms in which these questions came to be discussed in the subsequent history of social and political philosophy. Only Aristotle, who was at one time Plato's pupil in his protouniversity called the Academy, is at all comparable in influence. Plato's project was, above all, to restore respect for and adherence to traditional moral values that had been transvalued during the late fifth century B.C., the years of his childhood. In this sense he was conservative. Indeed, he felt that democracy itself was an aberration, the second worst of the five forms of political regime that he distinguishes and categorizes in descending order; only tyranny—rule by a single despot, the kind of government that he has Thrasymachus defend at the outset of the *Republic*—is worse. (The other three are: first, his own Republic; next, an honor-based, military-oriented type of government that closely resembles the actual Spartan constitution and that, like Sparta, falls short in Plato's eyes by not giving intelligence and the bearers of the highest wisdom, the philosophers, a dominant role; and next, oligarchy, or rule by the wealthy.)

At the same time, however, Plato felt that "the good old days" could not simply be restored as they had perhaps existed in Athens and elsewhere in Greece before the dawn of philosophy. Rather, the restoration of the old values must be undertaken on a completely new, thoroughly critical, reflective, and rational basis. In this sense, Plato was an extreme radical. The coexistence of these two apparently contradictory tendencies within the same coherent, systematic work—its dialectical tension, as it might be called—is the key to the *Republic*'s brilliance and to its importance. This characterization holds despite the fact that probably no one, not even Plato himself, has ever really believed that the type of community laid out there could ever be brought into actual existence as a whole in the real world. Probably only a minority of the book's readers over close to twenty-three hundred years have themselves accepted Plato's claim that that type of community would be absolutely *ideal*.

Beyond a doubt, Cephalus is meant to embody the good, old values in their good, old form. He is kind, pious, moral in every traditional way, a treasure trove of practical wisdom, for example, in what he says about proper attitudes toward growing old. But at the same time he is unwilling and unable to make even a stab at answering Socrates' very first, simple expression of doubt about the correctness, the universal applicability, of his conventional notion of justice and fairness. Thrasymachus, of course, embodies the vicious rejection of the old values by clever but irresponsible members of the younger generation. As noted earlier, it was a common view that Socrates had been just another such Sophist, as shown by the fact that an Athenian jury condemned him to death on charges of impiety and of corrupting the youth. The more personal side of Plato's intellectual crusade was to try to set the record straight by distinguishing Socrates from the Sophists as sharply as he could.

In Plato's ideal community, people like Cephalus and their descendants would go about their business of contributing, through the various trades and crafts, to the satisfaction of citizens' material needs and in the process realize a modest but limited accumulation of wealth. People like Socrates would be educated from infancy in an elaborate program beginning with "the basics" and continuing on through a period of military training, then university-type instruction with emphasis on mathematics and the hard sciences and periods of apprentice work in minor administrative jobs, on through the serious study of philosophy in its highest forms. At about the age of fifty, they would be fully prepared to assume top leadership positions as members of the team of Rulers.

There would also be a third group, intermediate between the business class (the overwhelming majority of the population) and the very small and elite ruling class, who would share in the early training of the latter but who, lacking their first-rate intelligence, would go to constitute the *military* caste. They would be superbly trained to defend the city-state, presumably the envy of all its neighbors, against attack. Both of the higher classes would live together in common, sharing common meals and common spouses. Plato speaks in this context of a community of wives or women, as well as of children, but elsewhere he takes great pains to proclaim his dissent from the dominant Greek prejudice in favor of male superiority. He argues that women, too, should be entitled to be Rulers if found qualified, although he believes that there will be proportionately fewer of them than of men.

Both upper classes, their basic needs attained by the work of the ordinary citizens, would be prohibited from private property ownership and from foreign travel. This total arrangement would be, for Plato, the ideal earthly embodiment of justice, which consists in everyone's doing the job that he or she is best fitted for. By contrast, he saw the messy quasianarchy of his own society as fostering incompetence and tempting brilliant individuals to go wrong by denying them the position of rule that should rightly have been theirs.

For Plato, order and moral virtue were vastly superior in value to freedom. He asserted freedom to be the supreme characteristic of democracies and, by that very token, an argument for regarding democracy, so understood, as a highly defective political form. The temptation to try to satisfy one's desires, which are unlimited and which, if given free rein, drag individuals and communities alike to the depths, is for Plato the basis of disorder and vice. Even ordinary people, who may not be able to attain to two of the four highest or "cardinal" virtues, wisdom (fully possessed only by the Rulers) and courage (the Warriors' special preserve), are able, in a properly organized society, to exercise the third, temperance or self-discipline. The fourth is, of course, justice itself. In order to ensure the general maintenance of order and virtue, Plato advocates strict censorship of artistic expression. For example, he finds the Homeric stories of immoral actions by the gods, which the Athenian envoys at Melos used to justify their conduct, scandalous and in need of elimination from the educational curriculum. Indeed, he holds art itself in low regard on the ground that it is far removed from reality.

Even the Rulers are to be considered as under constraint. This is so not only because of the prohibition against their owning private property, but also because, given the highly intellectual proclivities to which they will have been trained, they would prefer to spend all their time in intellectual pursuits rather than in affairs of state. But, Plato argues, the alternative to their taking regular turns at ruling would be for them to be ruled by intelligences inferior to their own, and that would be a severe penalty. He worries a great deal, in the course of the dialogue, about whether the Rulers will ultimately be happy, since happiness does seem to be the supreme goal of both individuals and societies. (Once again, as in the case of *dikaiosunè*, justice, the Greek word *eudaimonia* applies equally naturally to both contexts. In English, on the other hand, we find it a little awkward to speak of a community's overall "happiness" and are inclined to substitute the expression "well-being" in the social context.) At first Plato says (through the mouth of Socrates) that the happiness of the Rulers as individuals does not matter, since the well-being of the community as a whole is of greater importance. Later, however, he returns to the question and maintains that the Rulers themselves will be supremely happy under the arrangement he has sketched.

To someone previously unfamiliar with the *Republic*, it may seem passing strange that a book at once so profoundly dependent for its inspiration on the circumstances of a particular society at a particular point in distant time, and so marked by one individual's strong prejudices, should serve as the benchmark work for our entire long tradition and therefore be accorded such a disproportionately large space in this historical survey. It may seem strange in part because of one further aspect of the heritage that Plato has bequeathed to us, his fundamental philosophical conception of the nature of reality. For he was a very firm believer in the existence of ultimate Objective Reality, which for him consisted of a realm of *universal concepts*, beyond physical time and space, that English translators usually call the World of the Forms.

The Greek word for Forms is *eidea*, or Ideas, but it does not refer to what we today usually mean by "ideas"—thoughts in individuals' minds. Rather, for Plato the Forms are the most fully real and supremely true entities in the universe, and the everyday world around us that we perceive by means of our senses is but a distant and "fuzzy" reflection or partial imitation of them. Philosophical training consists in gaining insight into the realm of the Forms. Rulers in the Republic, having been given this training over many years, would thus be able to make their decisions in accordance with their firm *Knowledge* of absolute truth and not in accordance with any private whims or desires. Their subjects, on the other hand, lacking such training, will inevitably remain mired in the confused, ambiguous domain of mere commonsense Opinion (the *doxa* of Parmenides) or, worse, of Illusion.

In further explaining this belief in the *Republic*, Plato elaborates on his famous Myth of the Cave, according to which most human beings are like people who have lived all their lives deep underground looking at images of puppets projected by a pale light onto a screen that they are forced always to watch. They never even see the actual puppets, much less the real people whom puppets represent, and of course they never get to see anything in sunlight, much less the sun itself. Myth is the form of information that Plato regarded as the appropriate one both for introducing many profound truths to his readers and for conveying the most important truths to ordinary people, who have not passed through rigorous, disciplined philosophical training. Thus he espouses telling a "magnificent" foundation myth to the ordinary citizens of the Republic to keep them satisfied with their lower-class status in the belief that they are descendants of an inferior race.

Plato draws an analogy between the sun, supreme source of our light, and the highest Form, which he calls the Form of the Good. It is not a personal God, but it is at once supreme truth, morality, unity, and beauty—what came to be called "the transcendentals" in later Western philosophy. Just below the Form of the Good are the Forms of Justice and the other cardinal virtues previously mentioned. Only slightly below these and similar forms are the geometrical and other mathematical forms, which Plato also held in the highest regard. This whole scheme, so blinding (like the sun) in its apparent perfection, has left a lasting mark on Western thought. It founds the belief in universal, everlasting, perfect truths. This heritage may help explain why it may seem almost a desecration, much as a flag-burning does to some Americans, to trace its origins to a single man who was born and lived under very specific and somewhat peculiar conditions in a corner of the ancient world.

What does this apparent paradox, the fact that a very complex intellectual schema constructed and vigorously defended by one ancient Athenian male, whose writings happen to have survived, has been so influential over the vast Western culture to the present day, tell us about the history of philosophy and the nature of that culture? The reader should ponder this. Of course, just as Plato himself clearly made use of many prior religious conceptions, philosophies, and literary works in developing his own unique system, so his successors in philosophy used, reworked, and often simply rejected that system. This process began with Aristotle.

The first and perhaps most important difference between Aristotle's philosophy and Plato's concerns the location, to speak metaphorically, of the Forms (or forms, as it is more appropriate to write in Aristotle's case). Aristotle denied that abstract universal ideas existed in a separate, timeless realm and instead maintained that all earthly substances could be characterized as consisting of two components, their matter (the stuff of which they are made) and their form (the essence of what makes them distinctive from all other substances).

There are two additional types of explanatory principles (*aitiai*) that, according to Aristotle, can also be said to characterize all substances: their efficient cause (what actually brought them into existence, which is all that we usually mean today by the word *cause*) and their final cause or purpose. This doctrine, sometimes called the doctrine of the four causes, has a number of important implications for social and political philosophy. For Aristotle the form of the *polis*, the city-state, is its particular constitution or fundamental rules or laws, and the end or final cause of every political entity is the good life, what later thought often called the common good. Every political form, including even that of tyranny, or one-man rule, as long as it is not of the most extremely arbitrary and vicious kind, can and should be studied with a view to seeing how it can best function and be preserved.

Thus, while Aristotle shares with Plato the conviction that the study of politics has above all a moral purpose and dimension, he is more dispassionate, more encyclopedic, and above all, in keeping with his rejection of Forms as separate entities, more concerned with examining the evidence obtained by the senses in everyday life experience. He is known to have compiled, with the help of his students, a collection of actual city-state constitutions from all over Greece. And while his *Politics* includes a section concerning the ideal state, it is only a relatively short and incomplete final section. An earlier section, almost equally long, consists of critiques of various ideal state proposals, including Plato's, and of actual states thought by some to be nearly ideal, such as Sparta.

There is a passage right in the middle of Aristotle's *Politics* as we have it (the whole *corpus* of Aristotle's writings as they were bequeathed to later Western civilization consists of lengthy lecture notes, so we can only guess at just how Aristotle himself might have arranged or rearranged them if he had had a chance to edit them) in which he usefully spells out the various types of study that must be undertaken by the student of politics. By analogy to any of the other practical, as distinguished from purely theoretical, arts and sciences, such as physical training, he says, there are in the study of politics four kinds of concerns. These are: (1) the type of training or constitution that is best suited to different physiques or different sociopolitical circumstances; (2) the ideally best type; (3) the average best type, or, in other words, the type best suited for the majority of physiques or states; and (4) the type of training or constitution that is suitable under a nonoptimal assumption, that is, when the purpose is only to achieve something less than the best possible. (Instances of this last type of concern are the individual who wishes to be somewhat physically fit but is not an enthusiast and the city-state whose citizens wish only to muddle through with an inferior sort of constitution.)

The thorough student of politics must engage in all four types of investigation. This broad, comprehensive view of the scope of the subject matter would presumably include virtually all of what contemporary political scientists as well as social/political philosophers actually do. Indeed, the word Aristotle most frequently uses for the study that he is undertaking is best translated as science, though he also speaks of politics as an art or practical skill. This helps to account, given the enormous authority Aristotle's writings were to acquire, for the diversity both of approaches and of contents that in later times we collect under the rubric of social and political theory.

But of course the Aristotelian heritage consists of something more than, and different from, the mere advocacy of empirical investigation and of openness in subject matter. One central theme is his insistence on *organism*. This is the idea that the sociopolitical community is to be regarded as a whole made up of parts, each with its role to play, and each conducing, when the organism is functioning properly, to the good of the whole. While such a notion is already to be found in Plato, Aristotle places even greater stress on it and goes further in elaborating on its implications. Along with the idea of organism goes that of admixture, the insistence that well-run states consist of the harmonious interaction of diverse components: different classes and different governmental institutions. Here we can see the seeds of much later conceptions of the "balancing of powers."

Thus what Aristotle takes to be the "average best" type of state (the third of the four objects of study in the list that I have given) is what he calls a "polity." This is a state that is dominated by the middle class and that contains some democratic and some oligarchic elements. Thus, too, he criticizes Plato's Republic for laying too much stress on the unity of the whole at the expense of useful diversity. It is, he says, like a single musical beat rather than a chord. On the other hand, an organism that is too much polarized between two opposite kinds of components is, for Aristotle, just as undesirable as one that is too monolithic. This is the thought that lies behind his account of the causes of revolutions, which he attributes above all to excessive polarization between the rich and the poor classes in a given city-state.

Finally, all of this stress on the importance of preserving a middle ground in the sociopolitical organism refers us to another important doctrine of Aristotle's, which he makes most explicit in his work on ethics rather than in his *Politics*: the theory of virtuous conduct as consisting of a mean between two extremes, or what later writers were to call the Golden Mean. Perhaps the clearest illustration of this idea of Aristotle's is the virtue of courage, which consists of taking the middle way between excessive fearfulness, or cowardice, in one's conduct and the other extreme of rashness or foolhardiness.

Justice, too, can be subjected to a similarly based analysis. Aristotle does this at length in a section of his *Nicomachean Ethics*. There he brings out the close conceptual connection between justice and equality. He argues that different views of justice depend on whether one stresses arithmetical or proportional equality, "the equality of ratios." At the arithmetical extreme there is absolutely equal treatment of each individual, while at the other extreme there is entirely unequal treatment based on a hierarchical notion of differences in merit.

His complex and still very useful analysis shows that *distributive* justice, as for instance in the distribution of awards, makes sense only if it contains a merit-based element. On the other hand, justice "as *rectification*," as for example in compensating for an injury done, must have a strong egalitarian component; it takes no account of whether the injured person is a good or bad person, but only considers the extent of the (unjust) injury done to him or her. The contrast between Aristotle's and Plato's philosophical styles, or ways of approaching their subjects of study, is nowhere better illustrated than in a comparison between each one's answer to the question "What is justice?" Plato painted a magnificent canvas; Aristotle makes many subtle and detailed distinctions.

Probably Aristotle's single most important contribution to the history of later social and political philosophy, however, lies in his elaboration on a single concept he regarded as authoritative: nature (*physis* in Greek). True, he also wrote extensively about things that were "beyond the natural things" (*meta ta physika*, metaphysics). These latter include first principles and a rather abstract notion of God as immutable Prime Mover of the physical or natural world, but not a part of it. Aristotle considered the whole domain of human community as natural, the human animal being *by nature*, as I noted in the Introduction, social and political. He thus sought to reconcile a contradiction that had been alleged by some Sophist thinkers to exist between *physis* and *nomos*, nature and law or convention.

Customs and laws, these Sophists had pointed out, were relative to different communities and varied greatly. It was obvious, therefore, according to them, that laws were nothing but artificial products of human agreement. They are not based on nature, which is essentially the same everywhere. Aristotle's entire system, as far as its socio-political aspects are concerned, was designed to show that even the most diverse types of city-state exist to promote universal ends that are natural for human life. They are all governed by certain laws of human nature that are the same for all human beings. In fact, for Aristotle, the very institution of human law is eminently natural and rational for states, and the "rule of law" as such, which he defines as "reason unaffected by passion," is vastly preferable to the arbitrary "rule of men." The term, *natural law* is the short expression for this overall notion that was to occupy a position of preeminence in social and political thought for centuries and that still occupies such a position in the minds of many people today. Its origin is probably most accurately located in the *De Re Publica* of the famous Roman orator and eclectic philosopher Cicero,[6] but the notion itself is certainly Aristotle's.

Aristotle uses *nature* as a norm or standard against which everything in this changeable world can be measured. To act according to nature is to be good, whether our referent is a sound acorn that grows to be a healthy, flourishing oak tree or a child who is blessed with a proper education to virtue and grows up to be a good citizen of a good state. Conversely, to act contrary to nature is to be perverse or bad. Thus ethical and political norms are for him objective by definition, since the question of virtue is simply a judgment of fact, to wit, whether an individual or a community has lived up to his/her/its objectively determinable highest potential or has fallen short.

Obviously, however, individual thinkers' conceptions of what is and is not natural will differ. This is illustrated by one salient issue on which most of Aristotle's serious philosophical admirers of the Middle Ages, such as Thomas Aquinas, felt obliged to disagree with him: the issue of slavery. Early in his *Politics*, immediately following his effort to distinguish the political community from the smaller community of the "household" (*oikos*) and hence the art of politics from that of household management or economics (*ta oikonomika*), he asserts that some individuals are by nature slaves. He is very clear about this. Of course, he concedes that some people who actually serve as slaves should not be doing so, and vice versa. But he argues strongly against the position of those who claim that the institution of slavery as such is unnatural. He favors viewing slaves as mere human instruments who are not, properly speaking, members or real parts of the organic sociopolitical community any more than the mechanical tools used by workmen are.

It would be no exaggeration to remark that I, no doubt like most readers today, regard Aristotle's "argument" for slavery, based on certain presuppositions about what is natural and what is unnatural, as being simply "perverse." (This turns Aristotle's own language against him.) It teaches a lesson of skepticism both about the use of nature as a norm and, more generally, about the potentially insidious role of *seemingly* innocuous presuppositions in philosophical argumentation generally.

Property is one final topic of social and political thought for which Aristotle's emphasis on nature as norm or standard has had rich implications. He is critical of Plato's community of property proposal for the two upper classes in his *Republic* on the grounds that this is unnatural and would not work for long. (Aristotle is also critical, on partly similar grounds, of Plato's idea of nonmonogamous mating among the Rulers, but an additional reason for this latter criticism is Aristotle's reactionary belief in the natural inferiority of women.) Moderate property ownership, then, is natural for Aristotle, and simple money-making, which is part of household management, is a legitimate art, a quasi-natural extension of the natural practice of the trading or exchanging of goods to satisfy human needs.

But there are, from his standpoint, severe moral limitations on this pursuit. In particular he denounces the practice of charging interest on money lent as being thoroughly unnatural, since it is no longer connected, as the exchange of money for goods still is, with the original, natural human aim of the simple exchange of goods. This aspect of Aristotle's "natural law" position was to be adopted by the medieval Church, which in fact officially abandoned its prohibition of usury (meaning the charging of interest in general, rather than, as in current law, the charging of *excessive* interest) only approximately one century ago. It was strongly held, as well, by Martin Luther, in many other respects no great lover of the Aristotelian philosophy. Luther's bitter denunciation of usurers is cited with glee and a considerable degree of approval by Marx.[7] Indeed, Marx himself used Aristotle's discussion of the two kinds of money-making, and his related distinction between the use values and the exchange values of goods, as fundamental building-blocks in his classic work, *Capital*.

It would be a mistake to take leave of the ancient Greek world in this brief survey without insisting on the fact that its contributions to later social and political philosophy were as great (or greater) in some of its practices as in the theories of a few individuals. Thanks to its historians and philosophers, including Plato and Aristotle themselves, we have records of an impressive variety of ancient Greece's experiments with various forms of social and political organization, including many versions of democracy. It may have been inevitable that some of the most prominent philosophers, such as Plato, within these societies would stress their failures and inadequacies more than their achievements; for philosophy, as I suggested in the Introduction, is a preeminently critical discipline. But it is important not to forget that if Athens, as Pericles is alleged by Thucydides to have said in his chauvinistic but moving funeral oration, is "the School of Hellas,"[8] the wider Hellenic social and political world was certainly the school of Western culture.

A BRIEF HISTORY CONTINUED: STOICISM TO LOCKE

For the vast majority of social and political philosophers in the West between Aristotle's time and the beginning of the period of modern thought, and even for many thinkers since then, the influence of Christianity and of the Christian Church (or, later, churches) was overwhelming. This is not to say, however, that the whole period we usually call the Middle Ages was without controversy or interest for sociopolitical thought: far from it. Of course, as we have seen, there was considerable religious influence on the thinking of the ancient Greeks; both Plato and Aristotle were strong believers in the pervasiveness of divinity in the world. But Greek religious life, with its numerous gods and, beginning with the Golden Age, the large additional influx of mystery cults such as Orphism, with their secret rites and foreign gods and legends, from Egypt and the Middle East, was relatively free-form and very undogmatic. Christianity, on the other hand, began to place great emphasis on dogmas and credos soon after its very earliest years of existence.

Stoicism was one of the two major new movements, both Greek in origin, that dominated the philosophical life of the rising colossus, Rome, which had conquered Greece and most of the rest of the world of which Romans were aware and was experiencing its own literary golden age at about the time of Christ's birth. The other movement was Epicureanism (named after its beloved founder, Epicurus). Epicureanism was an ethical doctrine that advocated a materialist worldview. According to the Epicureans, the gods, if they existed at all, at any rate had no interest in human affairs. Along with this, they endorsed the gentle cultivation of private enjoyments or pleasures as the right way to live. Epicureanism as a doctrine seemed peculiarly well suited to a society in which the overwhelming majority no longer had any real possibility for active participation in political life, in contrast to those city-states of Greece which had boasted democratic constitutions.

Stoicism was quite another matter as far as its sociopolitical implications were concerned. It was based on the belief that everything, the entire vast world order or *cosmopolis*, is governed by impersonal, divine Fate and that the admirable individual is the one who goes along willingly, in calm indifference to personal pleasure or pain, with whatever the fates might have in store. Stoicism consequently laid great stress on doing one's duty, whatever one's station in life. Of the three best-known Roman Stoic philosophers, one was a well-educated slave, Epictetus. Another, Seneca, was an important adviser to Roman emperors during the first century A.D. The third, Marcus Aurelius, was himself an emperor during the late second century.

Stoicism served to support the commitment to political activity on the parts of those whom fate had placed in positions of political power, but not of those for whom fate had decreed otherwise. Its moral message, disseminated through a society that showed obvious signs of increasing decadence as time went on, was, unlike that of Epicureanism, in many respects congenial to the rising religion of Christianity. A number of Christian writers themselves recognized this. But in the last analysis its combination of a cosmic vision of a deterministic world order with the doctrine of indifference, *ataraxia*, gave no more encouragement to the spirit of radical criticism of the existing sociopolitical order than did Epicureanism. Thus it too should be seen as a symptom of decline in social and political thought.

Viewed historically without reference to its spiritual perspectives, Christianity was indeed a radical sociopolitical movement. It, like Stoicism and unlike most other prominent worldviews before it, advocated an ultimate egalitarianism: the equality of all human beings, male and female, aristocrat and slave, in the eyes of God. When it first reached metropolitan Rome from the Middle East, the majority of its adherents were from the lower classes. Yet, within less than three centuries it became the dominant worldview, and its institutional structure, the Church, was on its way first to dominating and then ultimately to replacing the political institutions of the Roman Empire.

It should not be thought, however, that the transition to Christian Church hegemony was instantaneous once the emperor, Constantine, announced his intention to become a Christian. There in fact ensued a long period of comparative chaos, marked by the repeated influx of waves of barbarian invaders from the East, many of whom eventually settled in the western parts of the old empire. The sophisticated infrastructure (roads, aqueducts, and the like) that had been developed by Roman engineers gradually declined. Eventually the seat of the empire, such as it now was, was transferred to Byzantium. And so on. One great writer stands out as epitomizing the spirit of this epoch and as setting the tone, more than any other single individual, for the dominant philosophy of the early Middle Ages: Augustine (A.D. 354–430), Christian bishop of the diocese of Hippo in present-day Tunisia, North Africa.

One of Augustine's two great works is his *Confessions*, in which he describes his evolution away from a life he later came to regard as sinful and pagan. The other is *The City of God*, which is of greater interest for our present purposes. This work has a number of different aims and is full of disquisitions on the most varied topics. Two of its principal aims are closely interrelated: One is to deal with the fact, then beginning to be widely observed by the non-Christians in the Roman world, that the rise of Christianity to prominence was coinciding with the decline of the empire. The other is to make a sharp distinction between the human political order that the empire had epitomized for several centuries (the City of Man) and the divine order. This is a heavenly kingdom with an invisible membership here on earth and the promise of eternal perpetuation in another world. To the question of why Rome fell, Augustine's answer is that God's ways are enigmatic and in principle unknowable to us, but that in any case Rome deserved to fall in light of its past wickedness. Only the City of God is of ultimate importance.

The tone of Augustine's reflections on politics is one that some later Christian theologians, notably Reinhold Niebuhr in our century, have designated "political realism." This involves a deep pessimism about the possibility of a morally acceptable political order and hence a rejection of most politics and most politicians. (This did not, however, prevent the Bishop of Hippo from overcoming his qualms and accepting the aid of the secular authorities in subduing the Donatists, a rival Christian group that at one time came close to achieving dominance in North Africa.) Without justice, Augustine asserts in one celebrated passage, kingdoms are nothing but large robber bands. Only in a truly Christian kingdom would there be genuine justice. There is, however, one passage in which Augustine praises the rare emperors who are truly Christian. This text had the value of lending his authority to those writers of the later Middle Ages, a period in which the authority of his texts commanded great reverence, who wished to be more optimistic about secular politics.

Finally, it is important to note Augustine's treatment of the issue of political obligation, the alleged duty to obey secular authority. He affirms such an obligation in the case of all laws and commands except those that go against God and one's conscience. This is an attitude that was to prevail among most Christian writers in later periods. But it can lead to very different behaviors and attitudes depending on circumstances and on one's interpretation of the precise meaning of the crucial exception. It is with this line of Christian thought that the notion of the importance of individual conscience, as in our contemporary notion of conscientious objection, begins to creep into Western social and political theory.

Prominent among the issues that Western medieval writers—all of whom, with the obvious exceptions of the Jewish and Arabic thinkers, subscribed to the consensus that the Christian Church and its doctrines were supremely true—fought over among themselves was that of the relative importance of the secular and the ecclesiastical authorities. Some argued that the hierarchial Church, centered in Rome, had ultimate jurisdiction even in secular matters. Others urged that there were large areas of jurisdiction into which Church authorities had no special claim to intrude. One specific form taken by this general dispute was the so-called investiture controversy—the question of the role, if any, of local monarchs or feudal lords in ratifying appointments of bishops and other church officials within their territories. In practice, there was sometimes confusion and disagreement between the representatives of the two legal systems, the so-called canon law and the local civil law, concerning which one should try someone accused of an offense in a given case. "Two swords," to use a metaphor generated (in A.D. 494) by an early pope, Gelasius, indeed hung over the heads of the men and women of this time. Only with the work of Jean Bodin (1530–1596), *Six Books of the Republic*, at the beginning of the modern age and the rise of recognizably modern states beginning with France, do we find a first coherent statement of the concept of *sovereignty*. It then becomes a technical notion indicating the clear jurisdiction of a central political power within a given geographic territory.

The most important thinker of the High Middle Ages, the period of recovery of culture and of many of the greatest achievements of medieval art and architecture, was Thomas Aquinas (1225–1274). His own work illustrates this process of recovery. The works of Aristotle, which had been known only very fragmentarily in the West, had been "rediscovered" through the increasing contact between the Islamic Moorish civilization and the Christians, who were busy reconquering lost territory, in Spain. Aquinas' teacher, Albert the Great, had played an important role in promoting the study of these works. Aquinas took upon himself the twofold task of assimilating Aristotle's thinking within a Christian framework ("baptizing Aristotle") and of considering the status of the large number of highly educated and often personally very moral individuals, the "Gentiles," who yet lacked all formation in Christian doctrine. Crucial to both of these enterprises was the notion of natural law, which received its classical elaboration at Aquinas' hands.

In considering Thomistic natural law theory, what is most important is its *rationalism*. Within a medieval context, there are writers whose tendencies are more voluntaristic (meaning that they lay stress on the force of God's sheer *will*, which is beyond human understanding, in effecting the way our world is). In contrast there are the rationalists who, while equally theistic in their beliefs, emphasize the identity between God's mind and what is supremely reasonable. (More recent forms of voluntarism and rationalism are not always or necessarily theistic.)

Aquinas' vision encompasses a lawlike world with a highest and most general level of laws applicable to all creation and a more specific level, that of natural law, applicable to and knowable by all human beings, not just Christians. Human beings are also subject to positive (laid down, decreed) laws of both divine and human varieties. Divine positive law is what is to be found in revelation, in sacred Scripture; it has therefore *not* been given to all human beings. Human positive laws are the varying laws of different states and territories, or what we most usually mean by "laws" in everyday discourse. For Aquinas, there may be problems with certain scriptural texts that require special attention (such as God's command to Abraham, testing him, that he murder his innocent son, thus apparently endorsing a heinously immoral act). And there are also areas of divine revelation that are beyond human ken (the "mystery" of the Trinity, for example). Still, there can ultimately be no conflict or contradiction among the various levels and types of law.

Hence a supposed human law that is obviously contrary to the universally rationally knowable natural law—in other words is demonstrably immoral—is to be regarded as no law at all. The rest of human law, however, is to be seen as part of the universal moral order. This natural law theory has the conservative function of ratifying existing political authority in a way that, while not overtly in opposition to Augustine, nevertheless shows a less hostile spirit toward politics. It gives a slightly new meaning to Aristotle's claim that the human being is *by nature* a social and political animal. At the same time it also contains a potentially revolutionary message in its insistence that any law and any political authority must be in conformity with the natural law if it is to be considered legitimate.

The Christian world's acceptance of Thomism, with its marked preference for questions about this world in which we live, in contrast to the previously dominant, otherworldly Neoplatonism, was not a smooth, untroubled affair. For example, many key Thomistic metaphysical doctrines were condemned as heretical in 1277 by the Faculty of Paris, composed of clerics. But it did not take very long for the general Christianized Aristotelian way of thinking known as Scholasticism (of which Thomism was one School) to conquer the field, so that Aristotle came to be referred to quite universally as the Philosopher. This is the case, for instance, in one of the important sociopolitical treatises of the late Middle Ages, Dante's *De Monarchia* (c. 1313), a plea for the unification of Christendom under a single monarch.

There was a sense in which medieval culture might at this point have seemed more complete and self-contained than ever before. But soon, indeed within less than two centuries, the whole of Western civilization was undergoing a sea change. Scholasticism was moving in the direction of a decadent dogmatism, the state in which Descartes and Hobbes were later to find it, by then in its death throes, in the early seventeenth century. The hegemony of the Church was being challenged by both secular and religious figures. Concern about political and social matters was being regenerated, both by the great renewal of interest in Classical thought and by many important discoveries, including Western Europe's "discovery" of the New World. (It is important always to remember, in view of the cultural imperialism of the modern West, that the native inhabitants of this "New World" had known of its existence all along.)

The *religious* side of the revolt against the cultural synthesis of the late Middle Ages is embodied in the pioneering work of Martin Luther. His Ninety-five Theses, posted on the door of the castle church in Worms in 1517, constitute one of the marker events of Western history. In the area of political philosophy, however, Luther's thinking is fairly traditional. For example, his 1523 essay "Secular Authority: To What Extent It Should Be Obeyed" reflects a "political realism" perspective quite similar in outline to Augustine's. The very fact that Luther's initial act of defiance took the usual Scholastic form of argumentation, the thesis, confirms the sense in which his revolt began as an attempt at Reformation from within the dominant existing cultural structures. A book written at roughly the same time, however, Niccolò Machiavelli's *The Prince* (composed in 1513 but circulated only privately during his lifetime), presents a more radical, secular challenge to the entire edifice. It is for this reason rightly seen as a watershed in the history of social and political thought.

Roughly midway through *The Prince*, Chapter XV is its "moment of truth." Up to this point, the reader of an earlier age might have been lulled into thinking that this was just another, albeit an exceptionally original, contribution to the time-honored collection of books of advice to princes, urging them to be pious and prudent in the discharge of their sacred, God-sanctioned duties. Aquinas' *De Regimine Principum* (*On the Government of Princes*), addressed to the king of Cyprus, is a part of this tradition. True, Machiavelli takes a special interest in the problem of "new princes" and newly established principalities or kingdoms, and this already suggests some departure from the traditional focus of such literature.

Then suddenly, at the opening of Chapter XV, Machiavelli warns that he is going to differ radically from what others have said. Others, he continues, have dreamed of republics and principalities such as have never existed. But his concern is to get to the real truth of the matter so as to be of use to those who understand. This "real truth" is that certain types of action bring praise and certain types blame, but the connection between the former and those actions that are morally good is by no means straightforward, people being as they are. What is important for princes in this world, he says, is to avoid publicly disgraceful vices that might lose them their states, but not to be too concerned about other so-called vices. Much of the advice that follows in the remainder of the book, with the exception of its final chapter, is in the same vein.

Machiavelli is clearly advocating a transvaluation of values analogous to the historical one described by Thucydides in ancient Athens. It anticipates that recommended three and a half centuries later by Nietzsche, who admired Machiavelli's thought. Leo Strauss, an influential mid-twentieth-century writer on political theory, and his followers have identified Machiavelli as the first in a series of thinkers whose "modern" outlook rejected the Classical and medieval view that ethical and social values are objective and knowable. This pits them against the Ancients in an epochal struggle in which the Moderns have so far tended to prevail, to the moral and political detriment of the world in which we live.

Others have seen Machiavelli as the founder of modern social science, defined as value-neutral *description* of social realities and of the techniques needed in the sociopolitical arena to get one's interests to prevail, in abstraction from all ethical considerations. This notion of social science owes much to the nineteenth- and twentieth-century sociological thinker Max Weber. It is probably less popular and more widely suspect now than it was a quarter-century or so ago.

Still others have praised or condemned Machiavelli, depending on their own perspectives, primarily as the first important, articulate modern spokesperson for the notion of raison d'état. This is the idea that, in political matters, the preservation and strengthening of the particular national state with which one is involved takes precedence over all other considerations, particularly ethical ones.

There is, as usual, some kernel of truth in all of these conceptions of Machiavelli. In the century or so following his death and the circulation of *The Prince*, his name came to be equated virtually with the devil. His little book was said to be read secretly by monarchical rulers, who eagerly sought its advice but did not wish to have this fact known. On the other hand, it is clear that Machiavelli's own views were more complex and more interesting than those of Plato's Thrasymachus, to which many of his critics would have liked to reduce him.

One way of approaching this complexity is to focus on the word *virtù*, which he uses frequently. Machiavelli wrote in his native Italian though he was familiar, like all educated persons of his day, with Latin. *Virtù* can mean skill, as in the stem of our Italianate English word *virtuoso*. For Machiavelli, the great prince is the person supremely gifted with the *skill* of statecraft. (He must also have in equal measure, as Machiavelli frequently points out, fortune or good luck on his side.)

But of course *virtù* is also linked with the Latin word *virtus* (virtue). This word had an interesting history, one of great importance for Machiavelli's purposes. In early, pre-Christian Roman times, it was closely linked with its stem, *vir* (man, in the sense of male human being). It connoted above all those qualities that a male chauvinist society would consider the "manly virtues": courage, particularly of a martial sort; honor; and a commitment to one's country. In short, it was the abundance of such "good old Roman virtues" (of which a few women were said to have had a small share, such as Lucretia when she committed suicide rather than face dishonor after having been raped) that the earlier Roman writers generally agreed was responsible for their national success. (Of course, the prominence of the Lucretia example in their literature speaks volumes about the sexism of Roman society.)

Later, with the gradual assimilation of Christianity into Roman culture, *virtus* was the word used to identify the "cardinal virtues" originally found in Plato's *Republic*, of which courage is one. This is taken together with a large number of more otherworldly qualities, such as humility, that would not have been a part of any pre-Christian Roman's list of virtues. Machiavelli admired the republican society of pre-Christian and pre-imperial Rome. (Julius Caesar, it must be recalled, had effected the transformation of Rome from republic to empire just a few decades before the birth of Jesus.) He felt that Christianity had brought about, or at least completed, the weakening of Roman society's moral fiber. This was evidenced by, among other things, Christianity's redefinition of "virtue."

In fact, Machiavelli longed for a return of his beloved Italy to a condition similar to the one that had prevailed under the Roman Republic. He saw the conquest and unification of the country by a single strong prince as a necessary precondition for such a restoration of republican institutions, to which the closest parallel in his own day was the ruggedly independent confederated cantons of Switzerland. He thought that such a restoration might come about, with luck, after a few generations of such strong-man rule. This is made clear if one reads portions of his much longer work, the *Discourses* on Titus Livy's history of Rome, together with the final chapter of *The Prince*. The latter is a highly emotional appeal for a military savior who would rid Italy of dominance by foreign forces. Perhaps the power of the papacy, which by his time had become enormously corrupt and subject to the influences of a few leading Italian families, might be used, Machiavelli suggests, to restore the country's lost pride and greatness. Ultimately, Italy could regain its freedom—a word he uses in a very positive sense.

The advice to princes to disregard conventional "morality" seized the popular imagination after his death. Yet it was his patriotic appeal against corruption and decadence and in favor of national restoration, with both prince and Church serving as means for achieving this end, that was Machiavelli's ultimate message. For him, as he wrote in Chapter XVIII of *The Prince*, in the actions of all men, and especially of princes, it is the *end* that counts (*si guarda al fine*).

In our brief chronological survey we have reached the sixteenth century and recognizably modern times. The times were also extremely troubled. The title of a small book from this period has become a household word in social thought. It stands as an ironic monument to its author as a victim of those times: Sir (or Saint) Thomas More's *Utopia*, first published in Latin in 1516. The word combines a Greek prefix and base word to signify "no place" or "nowhere." The book is an account of the customs and institutions of an imaginary island people who regard nature as their moral guide. They practice communality of goods without the use of money (although, unlike the higher classes in Plato's Republic, they live in households). Above all, they prefer simplicity to pomp and adornment. More presents the account in such a way as to be able at the end to express for the record, as it were, his personal disagreement with some aspects of the Utopians' way of life, especially their disdain of riches. But his admiration for these creatures of his fantasy by comparison with his English fellow-countrymen is clear enough.

It was a time, as the book's prefatory dialogue makes clear, of great upheavals and enormous public injustices. Foreign wars were being fought by large armies, capital executions were occurring in great numbers even for petty theft, and the relatively few with wealth were flaunting it shamelessly. Most tragically of all, landowning nobles and abbots were proceeding to enclose great tracts for sheep grazing, in the process depriving vast numbers of tenant-farmer families of their homes, in order to reap the large profits opened up to them by the rising wool industry. This "enclosure" movement, backed by royal decree and parliamentary legislation, was having the effect of creating masses of penniless vagabonds who roamed the countryside. "Your sheep," as More says, "that used to be so gentle and eat so little . . . are becoming so greedy and so fierce that they devour the men themselves, so to speak."[1]

More thus chronicles, although he of course does not call it by this name, the period of the dawn of modern capitalism. This was the same sequence of historical events to which Marx was to point, in *Capital*, as the violent origin (the so-called primitive accumulation) of the new economic system of which England clearly had become the leading exemplar by his own time. A little more than a decade after writing *Utopia*, More himself was appointed Lord Chancellor of England, a position he held for only three years. Compelled by his conscience to resist the demand of his king, Henry VIII, that he acquiesce in Henry's divorce and first remarriage and that he acknowledge the king as Supreme Head of the Church, Thomas More was beheaded less than twenty years after *Utopia* first saw the light of day.

England's troubles were by no means unique to it among the European nations as they proceeded on in their conquests of the Americas and their production of ever-increasing wealth. These continued on through the next century. It is probably not mere coincidence that the two greatest social/political philosophers of this period—Thomas Hobbes and John Locke—were both English. The key new concept of this period, central both to their writings and to a vast additional literature, was that of compact or contract, which has important overtones of legal and business transactions. The modern world of trade for profit and of voluntary agreements entered into on a basis of legal equality was rapidly replacing the medieval world of hierarchical religion, of unbridgeable differences in status, and of the chivalric pursuit of aristocratic "honor" for its own sake. The sociopolitical theory of the period was to bear eloquent witness to this transition.

The idea that political society is a kind of contract was not a totally new one in the seventeenth century. Hints of this metaphor are to be found in one passage early in Plato's *Republic*, in which Socrates imagines a primitive state, with a minimum number of members, engaged in the mutual satisfaction of basic needs. Hints are also to be found in the short dialogue called the *Crito*, in which Socrates, in prison awaiting the execution of the death sentence against him, is shown refusing the rather safe opportunity offered him to escape, through the payment of a few discreet bribes to jailers. He does so partly on the ground that by reaping the benefits of the laws of Athens over many years he had made a tacit agreement not to break them even when, as in this case, others had acted in violation of the laws to his extreme detriment.

There is even a certain contractual element in much of medieval and late Scholastic theory, including Aquinas'. Kings are generally expected to abide by existing customary law, above all the laws of royal succession; usurpers of thrones are held in very low regard. The Magna Carta of 1215 was a contract between King John and his barons. It formally recognized the distinctly medieval institution of representative, parliamentary government, representative at least for the aristocracy. And of course contract had been the topic of extended discussion among the writers on Roman law, the rediscovery of which had been an important stimulus to the revival of learning in the later Middle Ages. This Roman legal tradition, together with the tradition of natural law, was the most significant influence on one of the earliest seventeenth-century writers to use the notion of contract, Hugo Grotius (1583–1645) of Delft, in Holland.

Although Grotius believed that a real social contract existed between established governments and their subjects and created an absolute basis of obligation on the part of the latter toward the former, it is not for this aspect of his contract thinking that he is best remembered. Rather, he is generally considered the father of modern international law for his great work, *De Jure Belli ac Pacis Libri Tres* (*Three Books Concerning the Law of War and Peace*). This provides a systematic basis for international agreements and practices, in particular practices that are considered permissible in warfare. Grotius then goes on to propose another set of much more strictly limited practices that point toward the drastic curtailment of war and its ultimate elimination in favor of a just international order. To this day, Grotius' dictum *pacta sunt servanda* (agreements or compacts are to be observed) is generally regarded as the fundamental principle of international law.

But Thomas Hobbes is generally seen as the first great expounder of modern social contract theory. He was born prematurely, as he is said to have maintained, together with his lifelong "twin," fear, when his mother heard news that the invading Spanish Armada had been sighted in the Thames Estuary in 1588. There is no doubt that fear serves as a principal motivating force in Hobbes' social and political philosophy: fear of sudden and violent death on the individual level, fear of invasions and civil wars that greatly increase the probability of early death for individuals on the national level. Hobbes lived, part of the time in exile on the Continent, through the period of the English Civil War between the more radical Protestant Roundheads, led by Oliver Cromwell, and the royalist Cavaliers supporting the restoration of the Stuart family to the monarchy after the execution of King Charles I. Indeed, fearful as he was, Hobbes lived well beyond the Restoration, to the age of ninety-one.

Leviathan is Hobbes' best-known work. Published in 1651, during Cromwell's reign, it expands and sharpens ideas already expressed in an earlier book in Latin. In mentioning the biblical book of Job, I have already indicated the significance of this title for Hobbes. The supreme power on earth, within given geographic boundaries, is to be given absolutely and irrevocably to a sovereign, preferably a single individual, but conceivably also a sovereign political body. The sovereign, for Hobbes, is to be regarded as sovereign *representative* of his (or, he would concede, her or its) subjects, the citizens. The latter must be thought of as having made an initial agreement, usually tacit but occasionally explicit, to give all power and authority to whoever (or whatever group) is selected by the majority to be the holder of that authority. In other words, Hobbes' sovereign has supreme power over me, as subject, but it is I who have *authorized* (been author of) this sovereignty by my agreement to the compact.

Hobbes takes very seriously the metaphorical idea that a commonwealth is a "*body* politic," even to the point of including a famous drawing of a crowned male personage, presiding over a prosperous countryside with many homes and churches, and containing countless small people within his torso, on the frontispiece of *Leviathan*. Nevertheless, he breaks sharply in a number of important ways with the Classical-through-medieval notion of the *polis* or state as a natural organism directed to the promotion of the common good. He emphasizes again and again that this civic body is *artificial*—the product of human artifice or contrivance, central to which is the compact.

Hobbes' starting point is highly individualistic, based on an intellectual taking apart or *analysis* (a favorite word among seventeenth-century philosophers and scientists) of human beings that finds them to be, like everything else in our world, instances of matter in motion. Our fundamental motions, according to Hobbes' primitive behavioral psychology, are "endeavors inwards and outwards"—sense experiences that stimulate responses in the form of desires and aversions. For Hobbes, "good" is nothing but the name for objects of our desires and "evil" the name for objects of our aversions or hatreds. He explicitly rejects Aristotle's and many others' assumption that there is a "highest good" for human beings. However, he insists that there is a highest evil: death, the cessation of motion.

Hobbes thus angrily and often wittily attacks the whole edifice of Scholasticism: the idea that there can be any "spiritual" or "immaterial" substances (a notion he regards as an outright contradiction in terms), such as separate "souls"; the view that there is an objectively knowable realm of eternal values; and, as we have noted, the related sociopolitical concept of a preordained "common good." Typical is his terse comment in Chapter XIX of *Leviathan* concerning the claim that there are other forms of government besides the three that he considers the only real possibilities (monarchy, aristocracy, and democracy): "There be other names of government, in the histories, and books of policy; as *tyranny*, and *oligarchy*; but they are not the names of other forms of government, but of the same forms misliked. For they that are discontented under *monarchy*, call it *tyranny*."[2]

The idea of a "state of nature" or natural state of human beings outside of organized political institutions was already very much in the air by this time. It drew considerable force from the white colonists' encounters with the tribes of North America whom their geographical ignorance had led them to call Indians. Hobbes' famous conception of this state was to become a mainstay of early modern social and political philosophy. It follows directly from his behavioral psychological premises. In this common state, he imagines, everyone is basically equal. Whatever small superiorities or inferiorities some individuals might have can easily be neutralized or compensated for by temporary alliances. Everyone is fearful of everyone else while looking to advance his or her own self-interest and security. And everyone seeks what Hobbes calls "glory," or recognition from others and at any rate avoidance of their contempt. In this state of affairs, it is no surprise that individuals' reactions to each other are often hostile and even downright violent: sets of "endeavors outwards" frequently clash with one another.

The upshot is that Hobbes' state of nature is a "state of war," which means not so much unremitting actual physical hostilities as the perpetual *possibility* of them. In this state, life is brutal and short, and there is no opportunity to develop anything like culture or civilization. And if readers should question this somber picture of the natural state of mankind, Hobbes says, they should reflect on how many precautions we are forced constantly to take against assault, theft, and so on even in our own societies where some common force does exist to "protect the peace." Or again, he adds, consider the international scene, which on its own scale exactly reproduces the state of nature he has depicted among individuals.

As Hobbes analyzes it, the one positive thing that individuals have going for them in this state is their reason. He thinks of reasoning on the model of calculation, a glorified arithmetic using words in place of numbers. In fact, he structures his *Leviathan* in imitation of Euclid's geometry, using basic definitions in place of axioms and attempting to deduce later "theorems" from earlier ones. This reasoning shows an opposition between the obvious desirability of seeking peace whenever possible, which he calls the "fundamental law of nature," and the right to defend oneself by whatever means possible, which he calls "the sum of the right of nature." This includes the acquisition of whatever one may think desirable for contributing to one's self-defense. There then follows a second law of nature, which involves divesting oneself of as much of this "right to all things" as shall be deemed necessary for securing the mutual peace that reason has motivated us to seek. The "covenant" or compact giving absolute political power to the sovereign follows directly from this.

Hobbes later lists seventeen additional laws of nature, beginning with those of justice and "propriety" (property). These include an odd mixture of prudential precepts such as "against arrogance" and of such English common-law notions as "of submission to arbitrement" and "no man is his own judge." But his essential point about all of them, which gives them an entirely different force and character from the "natural laws" of the medieval thinkers, is that they do not impose any obligation on us whatsoever outside of a mutually agreed-upon commonwealth. Within a commonwealth, he holds, the interpretation of precisely what they mean and how they are to be enforced is entirely within the power of the sovereign to decide. Outside a commonwealth, he says, there is neither justice nor property.

It is difficult to overestimate Hobbes' influence on modern socio-political thought. To say this is not to deny that much about his own theory was unique, if not eccentric. With his individualistic view of the nature of human beings, he is often and rightly viewed as one of the originators of the broad liberal tradition that embraces many of those who label themselves conservatives as well as liberals within the contemporary American spectrum. Yet virtually no one in this tradition subscribes to his absolutist conclusions. His conception of natural right—that is, the right to everything within the state of nature—is as sweeping as one can possibly imagine. Yet no contemporary proponent of human rights would wish to endorse either this conception or the irreconcilable opposition between right and law that is its basis in Hobbes' thought.

His scripturally based religious views take up much of the second half of *Leviathan*, which relatively few students ever read. They are intended to reinforce the conclusion that the sovereign should be the judge of religious as well as secular matters in modern society, since only during a specific period in Jewish history did God directly intervene in an earthly political government. These views, I suspect, are not really compatible with those of any existing sect. Indeed, the argument over whether or not Hobbes was an atheist, as he was widely believed to be during his own lifetime, continues today. My own view is that he was a theist, but a theist of an extremely unorthodox kind, and that it does not matter much for purposes of understanding and evaluating his political philosophy.

Finally, Hobbes' views on liberty, while provocative and challenging enough, have won few adherents. His materialistic view of the world as bodies in motion leads him to analogize human freedom to the freedom of water to descend through a channel, the walls or banks of which at the same time deny it the freedom it would otherwise have to spread out in all directions. Just so, we are free to do as we please in those matters on which the laws of the commonwealth in which we live are silent. Thus, for Hobbes, there is no incompatibility between freedom and necessity. (The water is at the same time necessitated to flow through the channel.) Moreover, there is no incompatibility between freedom and fear, since the basic compact was freely entered into by individuals who feared deeply for their lives and safety. Hobbes thus undercuts the usual legal principle that contracts subscribed to under extreme psychological duress are not binding.

For Hobbes, more high-sounding but meaningless notions of "freedom" or "liberty" are extremely pernicious. Claims about freedom of expression at the universities helped undermine the royal power in England and thus led to the disastrous civil war. He even condemns his bête noire, Aristotle, for maintaining, like Plato before him and Cicero after him, that liberty was the foremost special characteristic of democracies. He does this even though, as we have seen, Aristotle certainly did not consider democracy the best form of government. The Ancients' talk of liberty, according to Hobbes, helped mislead readers of more recent times into acts of rebellion: "with the effusion of so much blood, as I think I may truly say, there was never anything so dearly bought, as these western parts have bought the learning of the Greek and Latin tongues."[3]

It is no wonder that Hobbes has often been accused, as has Plato despite the enormous discrepancy of their underlying worldviews, of sowing the seeds for and justifying totalitarianism. This is an oversimplification in both cases, but the fact is that neither was a great lover of individual freedom of action as a supremely valuable asset in a human community. For Plato, virtue, and for Hobbes, security took precedence.

The second great British social contract theorist, one for whom liberty was a very important value, was John Locke (1632–1704). His *Second Treatise of Civil Government* is premised on one central idea: that the end or purpose of government is the protection of property. He takes this term in a very broad sense to include "life, liberty, and estate." Although Locke lived as a young man through the same Civil War period in England that indelibly imprinted a sense of horror and aversion on Hobbes' mind and philosophical system, Locke's entire attitude, at least as we find it in his written work, is one of much greater optimism about human relationships and behavior. This is true for him both in the imagined state of nature and in actual "civil societies," as he calls all communities in which a compact to bind together and to create a mutually agreeable government has been made. Thus, in total opposition to Hobbes, Locke looks with relative equanimity even on the prospect of a revolution against a government that has deeply and repeatedly violated its "trust" (a word Locke emphasizes) with the members of civil society to which it owes its existence. After all, Locke says, a revolution may overturn a government without dissolving the fundamental compact of the civil society itself. Besides, he adds in defense of his doctrine, people do not rise up in revolt in response to minor provocations, but only when "a long train of abuses" makes clear the government's intention to act despotically. These words were to be echoed in the American Declaration of Independence.

The theoretical underpinnings of Locke's thought are in some respects quite ambiguous, and his own personal cautiousness contributed to this ambiguity. Some earlier historians of social and political philosophy, aware of Locke's very close connection with Lord Shaftesbury, a leader of the rising Whig party in England, tended to dismiss his writing as a mere political tract, a bit of sophisticated propaganda. It is true, after all, that Locke refrained from explicitly acknowledging his authorship during his lifetime. This was at least in part out of fear that the Whig Settlement or

Glorious Revolution of 1688–1689, which bloodlessly ousted the absolutist Stuart kings and installed a more limited, constitutional monarchy on the throne in the persons of William and Mary, would be reversed.

Later scholarship showed, however, that Locke actually wrote the *Second Treatise*, as well as the first, prior to that historical event. This appears to demonstrate conclusively that Locke's work was indeed based on strong conviction and not mere political opportunism. The seldom-read *First Treatise* had been written in response to an extreme and extremely specious argument for absolute monarchy that had been presented in a book called *Patriarcha* (1680) by Sir Robert Filmer. *Patriarcha* was based on an assumed delegation of the divine right of kings to rule that had supposedly been given by God to Adam, the first human being mentioned in the Bible, and passed on to his heirs. The crux of Locke's argument against Filmer is summarized in the final chapter (XI) of the *First Treatise*, which bears the wonderfully laconic title "Who Heir?"

Such absolutist claims appealed, unlike Hobbes' system, to supposedly traditional beliefs and religious values. They were in fact more commonplace and more absolutist during the early modern period of rising national states than they had been during the Middle Ages. In opposition to them, Locke's preferences are clear enough. He favors representative government and the location of sovereignty in what he calls "the legislative," with the Prince or monarch exercising royal prerogative to act, in trust, only in emergency situations when the Parliament is not in session.

Somewhat less clear are the connections between Locke's philosophical framework and the frameworks of Aristotelian/Scholastic thought and of Hobbes's, respectively. In Chapter III of *The Second Treatise*, "Of the State of War," Locke prudently distances himself from Hobbes' view that the state of nature is just such a state, although he does not mention Hobbes by name. Yet the answer he gives to his own question—"If man in the state of nature be so free, as has been said, if he be absolute lord of his own person and possessions . . . why will he part with his freedom . . . and subject himself to the dominion and control of any other power?"[4]—is not drastically different in kind from what Hobbes' response to it would have been. It is primarily the language with which the two philosophers characterize life in the state of nature—for Hobbes, a "state of war," for Locke "certain inconveniences," such as the lack of a common judge—rather than the substance of what they suggest such a life would be like on a daily basis that is worlds apart.

In addition, however, Locke insists from the outset that individuals in the state of nature are governed by "a law of nature . . . which obliges everyone."[5] It can, he maintains, be found by reason, and it teaches us that we are all the servants and indeed the property of our Maker, God. This underlying conception of human nature is far from that of Hobbes. Instead, it is redolent of medieval and postmedieval Scholastic thought, a connection that Locke himself helps us make by quoting repeatedly and with great approval from the work (*Laws of Ecclesiastical Polity*) of a Church of England neo-Thomist writer, Richard Hooker (1553–1600). Locke therefore wants us to regard him as being within the natural-law tradition. (In fact, in his younger years he had written Latin essays, which were rediscovered only in the twentieth century, in support of that tradition.) But critics question the conceptual compatibility between his assertion, as a political philosopher, of the existence of such a rationally knowable law of nature within us and his radical rejection, in his extensive writings on the theory of knowledge, of all claims that we are born with innate ideas.

What is most novel as well as central in Locke's thinking from a historical point of view, at any rate, is his account of property. It begins with a quite innovative perspective, which the Canadian writer C. B. Macpherson suggestively labeled "the political theory of possessive individualism." According to this, each of us is the owner of him/herself—of his or her own person. The account continues by maintaining that any extension of this self-ownership through exercising one's person, that is, through *labor*, justifies the further ownership of the matter with which one's labor has been "mixed." So, for example, by "mixing my labor" with the soil, and so on, as a farmer I create for myself an entitlement to the fruits of that labor as well as to the improved land itself. Of course, this works easily for Locke only in the case of virgin soil that has not previously been under anyone else's ownership. He always had in mind his picture of America, that still mostly unspoiled land. Leaving aside, as he conveniently did, indigenous peoples' claims, he imagined the whole world at the dawn of civilization to have been like seventeenth-century America.

Finally, Locke's "labor theory of property," as it came to be called, culminates in a justification of the *unlimited* acquisition of all durable property—that is, of everything that is not subject to spoilage. Morality obliges possessors of nondurable goods, Locke maintains, to share with others whatever they themselves cannot consume in time. But there is no such obligation in the case of durable goods. It is the latter, however, which have come to predominate within exchange and ownership relations since the historical invention of *money* in the form, usually, of gold or silver.

The veneer of commonsensicality that Locke cultivates very carefully in his writing overlies a number of tensions. His sanctioning of the unlimited acquisition of property (at least in the modern world) makes it easy to see why later commentators have viewed him as a prophet of early capitalism. It is in sharp contrast with Aristotle's opposition to the charging of interest on money and with medieval thought's insistence on charging only the "just price" in the selling of goods and its strictures against the amassing of great wealth. Yet the philosophical basis on which Locke draws his inferences is an abstract belief, common to all the early modern thinkers, in a fundamental *equality* of all human beings, which would seem to imply that drastic inequalities in property ownership are unjustifiable or at least require some special justification.

One way of reconciling this tension is that of "the Protestant ethic," with which Max Weber was later rightly to identify Locke. This holds that unequal entitlements to property are generated by hard work. But the obvious fact that property holdings in modern society are not always exactly proportional to the amount of work performed by the individuals involved indicates the unsatisfactory nature of this attempted justification. It is a problem that still plagues us today.

Moreover, a closer examination of Locke's writings reveals that his abstract theoretical commitment to human equality coexisted with an apparent rejection of Native American land claims and an apparent acceptance of purely male suffrage, of indentured servitude, and even of black slavery. For example, Article CX of the model constitution that he drew up for the Carolina colony reads: "Every freeman of Carolina shall have absolute power and authority over his negro slaves, of what opinion or religion soever."[6] Nevertheless, more than any other single prominent figure, John Locke, writing at the dawn of modernity, is the classical herald of contemporary liberal democracy. Recognizing the deep stresses and conflicts in this herald's own superficially successful synthesis may be a useful antidote to the deeply unphilosophical assumption that our current structures, having overcome some of these conflicts, are basically beyond criticism.

A BRIEF HISTORY CONTINUED: ENLIGHTENMENT, REVOLUTION, AND UTILITY

Although so much of Locke's theory has a special familiarity about it to American students because of its many similarities to the worldviews of the "Founding Fathers," it would be a mistake to regard him as the only important theoretical influence on them. Many of them were quite widely read in social and political philosophy. Of special importance to many of them was the work of the Baron de Montesquieu (1689–1755), *De L'Esprit des Lois* (*The Spirit of the Laws*). This treatise seeks to identify the principal underlying values in each of the diverse forms of political institutions: virtue in republics (or democracies—he uses the words somewhat interchangeably), honor in monarchies, and fear in despotisms. Montesquieu also devotes detailed attention, in a way not found in any previous writer, to the influences of geographic, climatic, religious, and other nonpolitical differences in accounting for such diversity. The idea that republics are preeminent in civic virtue was a firm conviction among the American revolutionaries of 1776, as it was soon to become among the leaders of the French Revolution of 1789.

France, Montesquieu's country, was regarded as the center of civilization in the mid-eighteenth century. Many of that country's best minds of the generation after Montesquieu's wittily satirized its backward-looking institutional structure (an absolutist monarchy, a decadent aristocracy, a wealthy church rife with superstition and corruption) while accepting their celebrity status as shining lights of its culture. The optimistic spirit of this so-called Age of Enlightenment both influenced and was influenced by American revolutionary leaders such as Thomas Jefferson and Benjamin Franklin. Indeed, almost on the eve (as it turned out) of the revolution that demolished its own pretensions to legitimacy, the French government contributed money and naval support that proved decisive in the successful termination of the American colonists' struggle. The formation of a wholly new republic that disdained aristocratic privilege seemed to vindicate the Enlightenment belief in the inevitability of historical progress. Here was, indeed, a "new order of the ages."

The most original and, ultimately, influential social and political thinker of the immediate pre-Revolution period was a wanderer who, while he lived for a time in the company of Diderot, Voltaire, and the other French *philosophes* (as the Enlightenment figures were called), remained in many ways an outsider among them, a "man from the mountains": Jean-Jacques Rousseau (1712–1778), citizen of Geneva. In Rousseau's *Confessions* concerning his adventurous but troubled life, we get a first glimpse of the darker side of the spirit of modernity, its deep anxieties. In his *Emile*, one of the Western world's most important treatises on educational theory, we see a sustained defense of childhood learning through experience in a setting that approximates as closely as possible to pure nature, uncorrupted by civilization. In a distinctive portion of the *Emile* known as the profession of faith of the Savoyard vicar, we find an impressive defense of a simple and relatively non-sectarian religion that emphasizes above all the reliability of the inner voice of one's conscience when it is allowed to speak without interference. Rousseau's culminating work of social and political philosophy is *Du Contrat Social*. Chronologically speaking, it is the last great early modern treatise of social contract theory. But its governing spirit, and in particular the sense in which it is so radically different from earlier social contract theories even while it makes a number of references to them, cannot be grasped without going back first to two earlier works. These are the "Discourse on the Sciences and Arts," which launched Rousseau's philosophical career, and the much more substantial "Discourse on the Origin of Inequality" that followed it.

A journal announcement of a prize essay contest happened to come to Rousseau's attention. The topic was "Has the reestablishment of the sciences and arts [i.e., the Renaissance] contributed to purifying customs [or morals—*moeurs*]?" When he read this, Rousseau had something approaching a nonreligious mystical experience. It instantly struck him that the answer should be no, quite the contrary, and his mind filled with a swarm of reflections concerning the evil, corrupting influence of what is called civilization. The essay, which won the prize, is more of a harangue than an argument. But it staked out Rousseau's position in contrast to the dominant Enlightenment conviction that scientific and other intellectual advances would inevitably make human beings morally better, as well as materially better off. It ultimately made an important contribution, as well, to the development of the vaguely defined movement later known as Romanticism.

The far more interesting "Second Discourse," which failed to win a similar prize five years later, was in response to the question "What is the origin of inequality among men, and is it sanctioned by natural law?" Perhaps the judges' verdict was influenced by the fact that Rousseau failed to speak directly to the second part of the question except in the briefest terms. He clearly did not believe that natural law in the traditional, medieval sense exists, and he thought it obvious that by the end of his essay he had demonstrated that social inequalities are thoroughly opposed to anything that could be called "natural right."

Droit naturel, the French term Rousseau emphasizes here at the end in contrast with the *loi naturelle* mentioned in the prize-essay question, can be given either translation, natural law or natural right, in English, depending on the context. Rousseau's political writings as a whole are a very important part of a general historical shift of emphasis from natural law to natural right. The latter notion finds its classical expressions in the American Declaration of Independence and the French *Déclaration des Droits de l'Homme et du Citoyen*.

The core of Rousseau's explanation of the origin of inequality has to do with the invention of property ownership. This in itself amounts to a very bold claim. Perhaps even more innovative is the method he uses to get to it: an imaginative, evolutionary philosophical reconstruction of human history, or philosophical anthropology. He begins by attempting to disarm potential censors dedicated to safeguarding articles of Christian religious faith—always a serious danger for writers in the early modern period. He points out that if one believes, as Christians are supposed to, that the Biblical account of human origins is factual, then one cannot also believe literally in the various philosophical stories about a so-called state of nature. Let us then "set aside the facts" (meaning the Biblical "facts"), he says, because they are not relevant to the question at hand. Instead, let us imagine human beings as they might have been in the earliest years of our race, not as they would now be if, already corrupted by all the learned behaviors of modern life, they were suddenly thrust into a world without sociopolitical institutions.

Our thought experiment will show us, he says, that our early ancestors must have been rather peaceful, asocial creatures, gathering their food from the forests and coming together, for the most part, only for purposes of copulation. They must also have been too dull-witted to enjoy much happiness. However, they would have had innate potentialities for sociability and self-perfection, along with the freedom to act to implement these potentialities. Eventually, after a long lapse of time, a period of communal living would have evolved. This would have been characterized by some inventions, by friendly rather than hostile competition, and by the cultivation of such simple arts as storytelling and dance. This, he says, must have been the happiest era of the human race. It might have gone on indefinitely, had it not been for the occurrence of some unfortunate historical accident that, for all our sakes, should best never have happened. Perhaps, for example, it was the discovery of the art of metallurgy in the aftermath of a volcanic eruption.

Whatever the details were, there followed a period of intense, hostile competition within and between tribes—a period corresponding to Hobbes' state of nature as a state of war. Inequality of possessions came into existence, and all that was needed to complete the triumph of inequality was a masterful bit of deception on the part of the wealthy possessors to convince the rest to ratify and make permanent this state of affairs through the formal convention of private property. Rousseau waxes eloquent here: The initiation of the institution of property was a "usurpation" that irrevocably condemned the masses to poverty and enslavement. The finishing touches, according to this gloomy account of human history as a downward spiral, have been added by the inventions of government and, finally, of absolute despotism. But there is, in an important sense, no turning back. In a long footnote, Rousseau responds to critics who might think of him as wanting to give up property ownership and go back to live in the forests with the bears. Most of us, himself included, he says, have become too habituated to "civilization," with all its evils, to be able to do so.

The Social Contract is Rousseau's later attempt to show how it may be possible to make philosophical peace with this historically irrevocable situation. Born free, he says at the outset, we are all in chains. While he is no longer going to try to explain how this state of affairs has come about, he thinks he can find a way of "making it legitimate." His solution is a social-contract formula that places the sovereign power in no single individual or group, but rather in the citizenry taken collectively and acting together as what he denominates "the general will." This is not to be confused with "the will of all individuals" taken singly and separately, each concerned with his or her own private interest. When a group of citizens unites to create a general will or, periodically in a general assembly, to reaffirm it, they are expected to place their private interests in brackets and to consider only the good of the whole. When they do this, they are by that very fact doing the right, ethical thing, exercising a higher and different type of freedom: "civic freedom," which is also "moral freedom" as distinct from the "natural freedom" of individuals in the state of nature. Of course, they may out of factual ignorance make bad strategy judgments in pursuit of the common good, but that will not detract from their virtuousness as sovereign citizens. For, he says, "the impulse of appetite alone is slavery, and obedience to the law that one has prescribed to oneself is freedom."[1]

In an important sense, although he himself does not use this term, Rousseau's theory is the first great systematic defense of participatory democracy. Since he is often cited, accurately enough, as saying that a democratic form of *government* would be suitable for a nation of gods but is not suitable for human beings, this claim may appear blatantly contradictory. Rousseau himself is constantly expressing concern, in various contexts, at the possibility of being thought self-contradictory. But in fact he had an excellent grasp, very superior for his time, of the dialectical tensions or paradoxes of human existence, and many of his apparent contradictions dissolve upon closer inspection of his claims.

In this case, it is important to understand that he sharply distinguishes the sovereign, which for him is indeed the citizenry acting as a whole, from the government, which may exist in many different forms and constitutes the practical, day-to-day executor of the general will. Ideally, he envisions small republics in which all citizens would gather at least annually or, if possible, more frequently, to decide general issues. Foremost among these is the issue of whether the present form of government should be retained. But specific details are to be left to the full-time government officials. Some of the Swiss cantons of his time and even much later operated more or less in this fashion. Rousseau also believed that, as was and is the case with his native Switzerland, the disadvantages of smallness in these individual entities could be compensated for by forming an overarching confederation. However, the portion of *The Social Contract* in which he would have worked out this part of his political theory was never published.

One of Rousseau's special concerns, which he shared with one of several earlier thinkers to whom he was especially indebted, Machiavelli, was the problem of establishing a new state. The mass of citizens who are uniting in a social contract to create such a state will undoubtedly, though pure of heart and well-intentioned, be on the whole fairly ignorant and unenlightened as to the proper course to pursue. Therefore Rousseau sees a need to bring in a visiting expert, a political wise man, preferably not a member of the citizen body, to propose a constitution. He calls this person the Legislator, or lawgiver. He invokes such historical examples as Moses and Lycurgus and notes, as Machiavelli had also noted, that founders of new states have often added to their persuasive powers by claiming to have received divine inspiration.

The word man is, unfortunately, the appropriate one for designating the Legislator. Rousseau, though he loved women both abstractly and, often enough, concretely, held strongly biased convictions about the superiority of males in most matters except virtue. This is made very clear in *Emile*, especially in Book V on "Sophie, or The Woman." His male chauvinist bias was not left unchallenged: in particular, it was very successfully dissected and critiqued by Mary Wollstonecraft (1759–1797) in her important essay of 1792, *A Vindication of the Rights of Woman*.

In the course of describing his Legislator, Rousseau makes a hesitant remark that constitutes an important break with a centuries-old traditional belief in the fixity and unchangeableness of human nature. This individual, he says, "must feel himself in a condition to change, so to speak, human nature, to transform each individual, who by himself is a perfect and solitary whole, into a part of a greater whole from which that individual would receive, in a sense, his life and his being. . . ."[2] It is language such as this that has contributed to the widespread accusation that Rousseau must be seen as the progenitor of modern totalitarian thought.

In a way, in this passage Rousseau is merely formulating, in more colorful language, the Platonic–Aristotelian–Thomistic conception of the state as an organism existing on a higher level than that of its individual members. On the other hand, his novel emphasis on changing human nature through the social contract in order to create a "higher" national entity can be seen as anticipating, however unwittingly, the ultranationalist cults of the state that have been so prominent during the past two centuries. Another phrase from *The Social Contract*, cited even more often by hostile critics, is "forced to be free."

In the context, Rousseau is saying that citizens who have committed crimes against the laws that they had voluntarily, freely agreed to respect merit coercive sanctions to restore them to conformity with their own initial agreement: They must be "forced to be free." In a sense, what Rousseau is maintaining here is simply the underlying, usually unspoken, working presupposition of any criminal law system,[3] but his paradoxical, contestative style arouses suspicion and, not infrequently, animosity. It is no wonder that the secondary literature concerning Rousseau's social and political philosophy abounds with the greatest imaginable diversity of interpretations.

One of the earliest and most destructive misinterpreters of Rousseau's thought was Robespierre, the leader of the French revolutionary government during the height of its bloody Reign of Terror excesses. He had read *The Social Contract* and came to see himself as the embodiment of the general will of the French people. Robespierre's victims were unfortunately not in a position to call his attention to the fact that he was misreading his author. This was the case with respect both to the feasibility of establishing a social-contract state in a nation as large as France—infeasible, so far as Rousseau was concerned—and to the possibility that the general will could ever be incarnated in a single individual or small group. The potential fate of every political theory, once published, is to be twisted into forms that would have been unrecognizable to its original proponent, were he or she still alive.

The French Revolution, initially greeted with enthusiasm by large segments of the educated and uneducated alike in Europe and "the New World," soon wore out its welcome with many as the executions of real or alleged enemies of the new regime became more numerous. Immanuel Kant (1724–1804), the great German philosopher who was widely seen as epitomizing the best of Enlightenment ideals, late in his life wrote a treatise, *The Metaphysical Elements of Justice*, that reflected this disillusionment. There he defended a liberal conception of law as consisting essentially of restrictions against others' interfering with or placing restrictions on my (that is, each individual citizen's) freedom to act. But he also upheld the conservative claims of political authority against revolutionary questioning, insisting that the very notion of a "right to revolution" involved a contradiction in terms. It must be remembered that in German, as in French and indeed other Continental European languages, the word for law in the general sense and for right is the same—in German, *Recht*. Hence, to speak of a right to revolution is to engage in apparent contradiction: It would be a right to overthrow right, that is, to overthrow the existing legal system.

It is rather generally agreed that *The Metaphysical Elements of Justice* is by no means Kant's best or most important work. Indeed, by comparison with his great work in metaphysics and epistemology, ethics, and even aesthetics, his contributions to social and political philosophy are relatively meager. This is true even though he derived great inspiration from Rousseau's writings and in fact made significant use of a formula of Rousseau's that I have cited. This is the dictum that freedom consists in obedience to a law that one has prescribed to oneself, invoked by Rousseau in distinguishing action on the impulse of mere appetite in the state of nature from the free action of a virtuous citizen in a social contract state. Kant took it as the key to his own central insight that individual ethics consists of autonomous, conscientious self-legislation of the moral law.

Kant named this insight the Categorical Imperative. It receives several different formulations in his ethical writings. The Categorical Imperative requires that we test any proposed course of action against the imagined world that would result if everyone were to follow a similar course under similar conditions. Would this imagined world, we must ask ourselves, in fact be a global moral "community" in which everyone treated everyone else with respect; that is, as an end in her/himself rather than merely as a means? Being moral, for Kant, consists in eschewing all actions that fail this test, regardless of whether or not conforming to such a rigorous sense of duty promotes one's happiness or self-interest.

Kant's single most noteworthy contribution to political thought, in my opinion, was his conclusion, mentioned in *The Metaphysical Elements of Justice* but developed at greater length in a short treatise entitled *Perpetual Peace*, that reason itself pointed to the strong requirement that there be no more war. This goal may be said to be the ultimate purpose of law, he held, and nations ought together to form a cooperative league to this end. That Kant, the supreme moralist, regards working toward the achievement of this as a moral duty is extremely significant. It is also consistent with the ideal of cosmopolitanism—the world as one vast *polis*—that had been broached by the Stoics and then widely disregarded over the intervening centuries before being revived by the thinkers of the Enlightenment. His proposal for a League of Nations was eventually—though, alas, not permanently—actualized in the organization bearing that name that was created after the First World War.

Among others who deplored the direction taken by events in France, few if any were as eloquent as a Member of Parliament, Edmund Burke (1729–1797), whose *Reflections on the Revolution in France* (1790) articulates the lament of a conservative believer in the value of historical traditions. Burke decries what he regards as the tendencies of the French revolutionaries and their intellectual progenitors, such as Rousseau, to try to establish their society de novo on the basis of abstract metaphysical principles without respect for their historical past. Burke romanticized that past, in keeping with his general insistence that feeling, or deep emotional sentiment, was worthy of the greatest respect and could not be reduced to clear and simple rationalist formulas. This latter view, without the accompanying romanticism in every instance, was indeed widely held in the late eighteenth century. It was, for example, shared by Burke's, Kant's, and Rousseau's contemporary, David Hume (1711–1776), who composed the famous dictum that, with respect to the foundations of moral values, reason is, and of right ought to be, the slave of the passions.

Like Kant, who owed so many of his insights (especially in the theory of knowledge) to the radical changes in his thinking wrought by a reading of Hume's work, Hume should not be considered significant primarily for his contributions to social and political thought. However, there are a few related matters on which Hume's views can be seen as embodying important developments in the history of social theory. For one thing, he broke with the still-dominant social contract tradition in his essay "Of the Original Contract." Here he invokes known facts about the historical origins of nations to argue that social contract theory is lacking in empirical basis and thus should be regarded as pointing to one possible foundation for government but by no means the only one.

In addition, Hume gives extensive consideration, especially in his monumental *Treatise of Human Nature*, to the origin of justice. He argues that this virtue must have come about *artificially*, unlike the "natural virtues" that are directly derived from the sympathy that we all feel for others. Members of early human communities, he speculates, must have come to a self-interested recognition of the mutual usefulness of having common rules of justice, as well as of property and promise-keeping. Thus, on the one hand, Hume rejects any interpretation of social contract theory that would deny political legitimacy to a state that has not been established through some form of contract. At a more fundamental level, on the other hand, he preserves the contract theorists' insistence that the rules by which human societies operate are based on conventions or agreements among the members rather than in the nature of things.

Probably the most important of Hume's contributions to social and political (as well as moral) philosophy as we look ahead to its later history, however, is the strong explanatory importance that he attached, particularly in his later *Enquiry Concerning the Principles of Morals*, to the notion of usefulness or *utility*. This idea, like that of the predominant importance of the passions and feelings, was beginning to enjoy widespread popularity by the late eighteenth century. It plays a central role, for example, in the highly popular book *On Crimes and Punishments* (1764) by the Italian jurist Cesare Beccaria (1738–1794), which pioneered in opposing capital punishment under most circumstances. The "principle of utility" received its most influential initial formulation, however, from the pen of Jeremy Bentham (1748–1832), who explicitly acknowledges Hume as the source of the term.

Bentham's motivation for his radical reformism came originally from his observations of the chaotic, esoteric, and seemingly irrational practices of the British legal system that he had begun to study at the age of twelve. He believed that "the principles of morals and legislation" (from the title of his most famous work) could at base be reduced to something very simple. His core insight was that pleasure and pain were the guiding determinants of human behavior, that human happiness consisted in the maximizing of pleasure and the minimizing of pain, and that the purpose of legislation and of the legal practices sanctioned by legislation ought to be, quite simply, to aim at achieving the greatest possible happiness for the greatest number of citizens. He was confident that a "pleasure-pain (or hedonic or felicific) calculus" could be devised to provide a quantitative measure of proposed legislation, legal penalties, and so on. In the area of penal reform, for instance, which concerned him greatly, this calculus would enable us to determine at just what point a given penalty for a given crime would have maximal deterrent effect, beyond which it would become excessive and lose its utility. His general idea gained great popularity and became a readily identifiable philosophical movement with its own journal, the *Westminster Review*.

Today, utilitarianism remains a very prominent part of the scene in social and political philosophy, and utilitarian arguments will loom large in later discussions in this book. From a historical point of view, however, there remains only one utilitarian thinker from the nineteenth century who merits special notice here, and that is John Stuart Mill (1806–1873), the son of James Mill (1773–1836), one of Bentham's friends and early followers. J. S. Mill passed through an early crisis that led him to conclude that the emotional side of his life had been relatively neglected both during his early upbringing as a utilitarian child prodigy and in adolescent years. He then proceeded, not coincidentally, to reject the Benthamite notion that a purely quantitative pleasure–pain calculus was feasible, since it is clear that different sorts of pleasures vary considerably in quality. Thus his book *Utilitarianism*, which did much to give a definitive label to the movement in popular consciousness, constitutes an important revision of the original insight.

Utilitarianism also confronts forthrightly the serious question of whether acting in accordance with the greatest happiness of the greatest number will necessarily always coincide with the avoidance of injustice. (Take the situation of a majority that, fearing negative repercussions from the authorities as a result of the activities of an innocent but popular public figure such as the historical Jesus, prefers to allow the innocent person to be punished for the sake of the putative greatest happiness.) This problem leads Mill to distinguish between the projected utilitarian consequences of single, particular acts and the long-term effects of making such acts into a general practice. It is the latter, he concludes, that must be given greater weight. Thus, while the short-term outcome of a single act of judicial injustice, even if widely recognized as such, might theoretically be favorable to the greater happiness of a majority, still the long-term consequence of tolerating a judicial system in which innocents were, on occasion, deliberately punished would undermine confidence in that system and the happiness of the majority along with it. This discussion anticipates, in interesting ways, twentieth-century debates over the relative merits of so-called act-utilitarianism and rule-utilitarianism.

Among John Stuart Mill's other important works are *On Liberty*, *Considerations on Representative Government*, and *The Subjection of Women*. The first is a classic liberal defense of the value of allowing individuals the maximum freedom of speech and conduct, as long as they are not engaged in harming others. Mill had a strong belief in the power of truth to win out ultimately over falsehood, and he argued that an atmosphere of openness would best ensure this triumph. At the same time, he espoused elements of what some twentieth-century thought would term elitism, warning in *On Liberty* against the dangerous pressures of mass public opinion. In his later work he urged that systems of representative government be devised in such a way as to allow more weight to the opinions of the educated than of the uneducated.

Particularly innovative and controversial for its time, incredible as this may seem to us who are a mere century and a quarter's remove from it, is Mill's forceful argument in favor of (comparative) equality for women, including their being accorded voting rights. His ideas on this subject were largely shaped by Harriet Taylor (1807–1858), with whom he early formed a lifelong intellectual friendship that culminated in seven years of marriage after the death of her first husband, ending in her own early death. While they shared many values and ideas, including a firm belief in human moral progress, there is evidence that Harriet Taylor was the more "radical" of the two. She espoused work possibilities outside the home even for married women (a position Mill did not accept) and appears to have contributed to his moving away from a pure laissez-faire ideology and toward acceptance of the possibility of some measure of socialism in later editions of his *Principles of Political Economy*. *The Subjection of Women* was written shortly after Harriet Taylor's death, but Mill did not consider the time ripe for its publication, in view of the strong current of popular prejudice against the ideas it contained, until 1869.

In short, even those figures, such as Kant and Mill, whom historians associate most closely with the period of so-called Enlightenment and the increasingly widespread post-Enlightenment belief in inevitable human progress were often confronted with very unenlightened fellow citizens, as in Mill's case, and political authorities, as in Kant's. (Kant, for instance, abided by the prohibitions of an official censor until the death of the king that censor had served.) The heady, widespread inference that the French and American revolutions together marked decisive turning points in the history of the human race encounters serious reality checks when one considers the Reign of Terror and then the Reaction of Thermidor that followed the former and the brutal practices of black slavery and dispossession of indigenous peoples from their lands that continued to thrive for decades after the latter. Mill's "progressive" nineteenth century was also the great age of European imperialism. Nevertheless, it is certainly true that many radically new and often promising social and political institutions were created during this entire period. At the same time, certain philosophers were beginning to treat with seriousness the relevance for social and political thought of the data of history itself, once scorned by Aristotle as a study without philosophical significance.

A BRIEF HISTORY CONCLUDED: FROM HEGEL TO THE TWENTIETH CENTURY

It is now appropriate to retrace our steps back in time from Mill's generation and, initially, across the North Sea from England to the Continent in order to take account of Germany's two giant thinkers of the early and mid-nineteenth century, Georg Wilhelm Friedrich Hegel (1770–1831) and Karl Marx (1818–1883). Both have in common with Hegel's intellectual forebear Kant an antipathy to utilitarianism, although their reasons for this antipathy differ. Central to the categorical imperative doctrine of Kantian ethics was the idea that the morality or immorality of any proposed conduct is a totally different issue from that of its likelihood of producing or not producing happiness. In a Kantian ethic of duty, Mill's problem of having to explain why it would be improper to punish an innocent person even if this would make the vast majority of the population very happy never arises.

Hegel, in his *Phenomenology of Mind* (or *Spirit*), focuses less on utilitarianism's strictly ethical implications. Rather, he sees the principle of utility as the reductio ad absurdum endpoint of the thought of the Enlightenment, distilling the whole richness of human worth into a simple, abstract idea that cannot be incorporated within human subjectivity. (Hegel's argument for this is that the greatest happiness of the greatest number is described as an objectively measurable phenomenon that is in principle beyond any individual's personal grasp or control.) The collapse, as Hegel sees it, of the Enlightenment/utilitarian attitude leads directly to a worldview that advocates "absolute freedom," destroying all traces of the past as well as all respect for human individuality and subjectivity, thus sanctioning the boundary-less slaughter known as the Terror.

In an important respect, then, the mature Hegel's estimate of the French Revolution, which he had greeted with enthusiasm along with most of his schoolmates when he had first learned of it, is identical with Burke's. There is even some parallel, in Burke's *Reflections on the Revolution in France*, with Hegel's linkage of the Revolution with utilitarianism, as when the former intones his famous lament: "The age of chivalry is gone. That of sophisters, economists, and calculators has succeeded, and the glory of Europe is extinguished forever."[1] But, as we shall soon see, Hegel's view of post-Revolutionary Europe, elaborated more than thirty years later, is much more optimistic than Burke's.

Marx will have little to say by way of direct critique of utilitarian thinking. He did meet and converse with John Stuart Mill after moving from Germany to London, but was apparently not greatly impressed by him. There is, however, a crucial passage referring to the founder of utilitarianism in Marx's classic, *Capital*. Here, with deep sarcasm, Marx summarizes the supposed virtues of the capitalist system as it appears on the surface, in its day-to-day mode of buying and selling commodities, just prior to the in-depth analysis that is intended to bring out its inherently necessary exploitation of the working class. It reads in part:

This sphere that we are deserting . . . is in fact a very Eden of the innate rights of man. There alone rule Freedom, Equality, Property, and Bentham. Freedom, because both buyer and seller . . . are constrained only by their own free will. . . . Equality, because . . . they exchange equivalent for equivalent. Property, because each disposes only of what is his own. And Bentham, because each looks only to himself.[2]

The liberal individualism that Marx satirizes here and that is so fundamental to utilitarian thinking is, for both Hegel and Marx, a distortion of both sociopolitical reality and sociopolitical ideals. The point about which they diverge most drastically, beyond their shared objects of philosophical criticism and their shared dialectical methodology, is the site or location of the sociopolitical ideal. For Hegel, the ideal lies in the modern nation-state when properly understood apart from its minor, incidental warts and dysfunctions. For Marx, on the contrary, it lies in a radically different possible future "society of associated producers" after the present order has collapsed from its own internal contradictions.

Hegel is among history's most thoroughly systematic and encyclopedic philosophers, comparable in this respect to Aristotle, whose work he greatly respected. One could perhaps identify, without too much oversimplification, the greatest single difference between them as being Hegel's stress on the centrality of change across time, as compared to Aristotle's belief in the fixity of species. A half-century before Darwin's work burst upon the historical scene, then, Hegel may be said to have contributed importantly to evolutionary thinking.

But the evolution in which Hegel was most interested was that of the human spirit rather than that of biology. His first and most significant major book was his *Phänomenologie des Geistes* (*Geist* is translatable as either "mind" or "spirit"), completed in a rush when Hegel found himself forced to flee from the city of Jena as Napoleon's army was approaching to wage a decisive battle in its campaign of conquest. This book attempts systematically to trace various logical stages of human consciousness, from that of the simplest and most credulous belief in the truth of immediate sense data, on up through levels of complexity that culminate in the spirit of modern religious community and, beyond that, in a brief, systematic philosophical reconstruction of all of the earlier stages that Hegel calls "absolute knowledge." This final perspective supposedly constitutes our own point of view once we have read his book with full comprehension and have come to see its truth.

The scope of Hegel's claim here is of course breathtaking in its arrogance, but Hegel was sincerely convinced that he was living at a time at which human history had reached its point of culmination. In this regard, the juxtaposition between his thought and the figure of Napoleon, whom Hegel saw riding on horseback, was by no means coincidental. For Napoleon, to Hegel, was the latest of the rare "world-historical individuals" who, at various moments in history, have served as vehicles for the self-realization, through time, of Spirit, which Hegel considers to be at once both humankind taken collectively and God. From a theoretical point of view, it came as no great surprise to Hegel to learn that Napoleon, less than a decade after his triumph at Jena, had been banished to permanent exile on the island of St. Helena. World-historical individuals, great as they are, are in the last analysis only vehicles of a higher purpose, and their lives have usually ended in personal tragedy and defeat. (Alexander the Great and Julius Caesar are two other examples cited by Hegel.)

What was important to Hegel about Napoleon was not his apparent charisma, his military skill, or, certainly, his connection with French nationalism. Rather, it was the sense in which Napoleon epitomized a certain spirit of modernity. Among his achievements that, to Hegel, best exemplified this was his success in forcing most of Europe (England, never conquered by him, being the outstanding exception) to scrap its outmoded common-law systems in favor of code law. Napoleon also contributed enormously to German unification by eliminating scores of the small, independent political entities that had existed there prior to his conquests. It would have been no surprise to Hegel to learn that France itself would ultimately suffer greatly, during the ensuing period of more than a century, from a now-unified Germany. History, for Hegel, is full of "counter-finalities" wherein the original purposes of the initiators of chains of events become turned around and often produce outcomes opposite to what had been intended.

The dense and difficult *Phenomenology of Spirit* is meant by Hegel to present an ordered logical sequence of stages of human consciousness as such, with only incidental illustrative references to historical incarnations of particular stages, such as the Enlightenment—utility—absolute freedom—Terror sequence cited previously. His *Philosophy of History*, on the other hand, attempts to present world history as an actual realization of God's purposes. Its basic schema is relatively simple. The supreme purpose of human history, for Hegel, has been the ever-deeper realization of *freedom*, which finds its fullest and most complete realization in the modern state of the nineteenth century.

World history, according to Hegel, has consisted of four important phases: the Oriental world, the Greek world, the Roman world, and the world of modern Germanic (Western European) civilization. These phases have been characterized by three different stances (the Greek and Roman worlds being the same in this respect) toward freedom: One is free, some are free, all are free. The ancient East, which encompasses many different civilizations such as, for example, the Persian, was in general dominated by despotic governments, which allowed only the despot himself to have his way freely and treated all of the subjects as in some sense his slaves. The Greek world, for which Hegel had enormous admiration, introduced the notion of the free citizen, but it was built on and maintained by the institution of slavery. Aristotle's dictum that some are by their nature free and some are by nature slaves served as the inspiration for Hegel's entire schema.

The Roman world, which also had slavery, represents in many ways a historical retrogression, especially during the long period of the Empire. For Hegel, the Roman civilization was a comparatively soulless one, in which the only acceptable notion of "personality" was the objective status one had within a set of formal, legal relationships. Nevertheless, Rome constitutes a necessary stage in history, too. Roman law, for all its flaws, is an important advance, and the climate of the Roman Empire was conducive to the introduction and eventual triumph, after centuries of persecution and struggle, of Christianity. Christianity itself has required centuries of often discouraging and repressive development to reach its modern stage. But it has always contained within itself the insights of universal human equality and of the rich, deep capacities for the subjective self-development of every human person within his/her community that now serve as the basis for the genuinely, universally free civilization of modern times.

One may well ask what is to be said about all the countries and even continents that go unmentioned in Hegel's grand narrative of what World History (capitalized) has "really" been up to his time.

His answer, essentially, is that they simply have not counted, even though the inhabitants of some of them have probably been happier than the inhabitants of those who have played center stage. It is the latter who have been, as a matter of straightforward fact, central to the self-unfolding of Spirit across time.

One may also wonder whether, as many fatuous commentators have claimed, Hegel honestly believed that "history had come to an end" (a notion that experienced a curious revival in the United States in late 1989). Whatever sentences in his texts may suggest this, they must be understood within the context of a rigid limitation that Hegel placed on his own thought and would have liked other philosophers to observe as well. Philosophy, he felt, can only reconstruct, conceptually, what has happened so far and is happening now; it can in no way pretend to predict the future. Thus, from his perspective in the 1820s, history appeared to have reached a definitive culmination, and that is all that he felt it permissible to write as a systematic philosopher. In a few offhand remarks in the *Philosophy of History*, however, he shows that he expects history's then-current period of Eurocentrism to be succeeded by the rise of the Americas, especially North America, and perhaps Russia. As Napoleon himself said, and Hegel quotes him, "*Cette vieille Europe m'ennuie*" ("this old Europe bores me").

Although it should already be quite clear that Hegel's philosophy of history must have an important bearing on his social and political thought, Hegel himself makes the connection very explicit in the final pages of his *Philosophy of Right* (or *Law*). This work, one of the foremost classics in the history of Western political thought, concludes by asserting that the entire, complex structure of the modern state, which it has been the purpose of the whole book to present in idealized form, is itself subject to the "judgment" of "the Court of World History." Hence (so the obvious implication goes) it will eventually give way to something else. The book's conclusion briefly recapitulates Hegel's stages of world history.

The *Philosophy of Right* is divided into three main sections: Abstract Right, Morality, and *Sittlichkeit*. *Sittlichkeit* means, roughly, social ethics, in contrast to morality considered from the standpoint of the individual, as the latter is found in Kant's ethical thought. As is characteristic of Hegel's dialectical method as he utilizes it throughout his writings, this triadic schema is intended to depict increasingly concrete (decreasingly abstract), increasingly rich, comprehensive, and all-sided perspectives on its subject matter. A few additional remarks about this methodology may be in order here.

There is a sense in which the second of the three "moments" of a Hegelian triad stands in sharp contradiction or "negation" to the point of view of the first moment, while the third, more adequate than either of the first two, manages both to incorporate and to advance beyond both of them. The standard thesis—antithesis—synthesis formula, used by some philosophers and commentators to attempt to capture the essence of dialectical triadicity, is clearly misleading, since the third moment is more than just a synthesis of the first two, instead going beyond them. The expressions *negation* and *negation of the negation* come closer to describing the functions of moments two and three, respectively.

In any case, as Hegel frequently remarks, any abstract formula is bound to be distortive; one has to follow in detail the particular dialectical sequence in question in order to comprehend just why one "moment" must, if he is correct, inevitably give way, by virtue of its own internal inadequacy, to the next. Dialectics can best be characterized in contrast to its opposite, analytical reasoning, the method Hegel sometimes calls that of "the mere understanding." The latter sees reality only atomistically rather than wholistically, and takes history, for example, to be "just one damned thing after another" rather than the coherent tapestry of sequential events that it was for Hegel.

This methodological background is essential for interpreting the significance of Hegel's ordering of topics in the *Philosophy of Right*. Abstract Right, the first topic, corresponds, for Hegel, to the stage of taking possession of things, formalizing the possession of them as property ownership, and contractually buying and selling them and risking their loss through fraud or physical force. The later social contract theorists (Locke, Rousseau, and others) considered this stage to be possible prior to the establishment of more organized society and, eventually, of government. Hegel himself does not accept social contract theory and in fact at one point indicts it, especially in the person of Rousseau, for having contributed to the occurrence of the French Revolution by mistakenly maintaining that what is essentially a commercial-type arrangement could serve as an adequate underpinning for something as majestic as the state.

However, he is committed to showing at all times that even the most mistaken views of previous philosophers have some place when properly understood within the true order of things. Thus the topics dealt with under "abstract right," a sphere that by itself and apart from the higher levels of sociopolitical organization is, as Hegel shows, extremely unstable, do play a significant role in his theory. Above all, in this section, Hegel stresses that the ownership of *some* property, as even the fact that Locke's labor theory of property began by asserting that I own property in my own person may dimly suggest, is necessary for one to be a genuine person, a full-fledged member of human society.

Just how much a given individual owns is, according to Hegel, an unimportant detail. Moreover, he considers the fact that wage-earners do not own their own time, so to speak, during the period of their working day and proceeds to dismiss any suggestion that this might somehow detract from their full personhood. Only slavery, not any other inequality among members of society in the workplace, is ruled out by his position. Marx will, of course, take drastic exception to this facile dismissal of the significance of "wage slavery."

The second part of the *Philosophy of Right*, Morality, is by far the shortest and occupies a somewhat ambiguous position within it. Perhaps most interesting about it in light of earlier social and political theory is the extent to which Hegel focuses, in criticizing the standpoint of the ethics of the individual, on the appeal to individual conscience that was so strong in Kant's ethics and in Rousseau's *Emile*. The problem with such an appeal, Hegel points out, is that there is by definition no way of checking it, so that it must always be on the border of fanaticism and downright evil. The point of this entire criticism is that an ethical outlook is ultimately sustainable only within the shared values of some *community* or other. This leads him to the third part, *Sittlichkeit*.

There is a triadic division within this section as well: family, civil society, and state. The brief discussion of family recalls the Antigone story and Aristotle's mention of the historical evolution from tribes to the *polis* at the beginning of his *Politics*. In the modern world, the family exists to nourish the individual as a child. Male children (Hegel, whose personal relationships with women were more conventional in the modern sense than those of most male philosophers before him, never wavered in his belief that women's proper sphere was the home) must then move out from the family into the business world, the world of civil society. His treatment of this next sphere is the most interesting and important of the book. It reveals important linkages between past thinkers such as Locke and later thinkers such as Marx, and it also makes connections with the "real world" of capitalist economic relationships that was by this time clearly coming of age in Great Britain, France, and the Low Countries, and, though more tardily, Germany itself.

Hegel is intentionally ambivalent about civil society as he depicts it. Its organization—in other words, the organization of commerce and industry—is designed systematically to satisfy human needs in the modern world. He notes that an entire, quite remarkable science—that of political economy as developed by Adam Smith, David Ricardo, and others—has arisen to furnish an explanation of it. But what this science provides, he continues, is just a "show" of rationality, an analytical explanation that meets the demands of "mere understanding" but that cannot be the whole story about our life in society.

This *bürgerliche Gesellschaft* ("bourgeois society" in another translation) is the domain in which selfish, private interests are rightly expected to find full expression and to clash with one another in competition in the market, which, according to Smith, achieves some ultimate balance and harmony through a mysterious mechanism. But this hardly amounts, Hegel indicates, to genuine, positive human community. Locke was therefore mistaken to take "civil society" as the basic realm for human social life, with government existing merely to safeguard the private interests of individual property owners.

Moreover, Hegel claims that an internal dialectic within civil society results in the relegation of a certain portion of the population to a standard of living below subsistence levels, even while great wealth is being created at the top. This results in systems of poor relief that are frequently quite inadequate (as, for example, in England) for this "penurious rabble" and ultimately in a particular civil society's going beyond its borders to seek markets in underdeveloped countries. This portion of Hegel's treatment of civil society is a remarkable anticipation, within a few pages, of the general outline of Marx's conception of the dynamics of capitalism.

But Hegel then goes on to find a reconciliation of all the crudities and contradictions of civil society at the level of the state. The institutional structure he describes here bears considerable resemblance to the Prussian state of his day, the state for which, by the time of publication of the *Philosophy of Right*, he served as official philosopher in his capacity as occupant of the academic chair at the University of Berlin. It was, in effect, a constitutional monarchy, although during a period of reaction that began shortly after Hegel's death the monarch became more powerful again and the "constitutional" aspects were diminished. The details of Hegel's philosophical reconstruction of the state can be omitted here, except to note his wish to confine the monarch to a crucial but subsidiary role, that of providing a necessary "personal touch" of approval to legislation. This seems clear from the fact that he treats "the Crown" as only the first moment, rather than the last, in the triadic constitutional structure as he outlines it.

Hegel's assertions about the importance of the state—"the actuality of the ethical Idea," the embodiment of freedom, which has a supreme claim on the allegiance of individuals living with it—are truly grandiloquent and even, especially in light of later events, frightening. This impression is hardly mitigated by the fact that, near the end of his discussion of *Sittlichkeit*, he defends the value of war for forcefully bringing out the evanescence and contingency of individual human life and property and for permitting the virtue of courage to be realized more fully. Then, just before his summary of world history as the court of judgment, he dismisses international law as a mere ought-to-be, although having some slight importance in regulating the rules of warfare. He discounts Kant's League of Nations proposal as being always dependent on the contingent good will of individual sovereign states.

That later nineteenth-century German nationalists and early-twentieth-century Italian nationalists would use Hegel's work in advocating a strong cult of the state is therefore no wonder. But in doing so they glossed over the many significant features of his political thought that militate against ultranationalism. They also neglected, in large measure, the background of the dialectical view of reality and in particular of history against which his excessively adulatory statements about the state in the *Philosophy of Right* must be placed.

Marx came to Berlin as a student shortly after Hegel's death, when the Hegelian system was still central to most discussions about contemporary philosophy. He therefore felt an obligation to come to grips with it. A rift was already beginning to take place between the so-called Left and Right Hegelians, with questions about the theological implications of Hegel's thought serving as the prime point of contention between them. Hegelians of the Right tried to defend the compatibility of Hegelianism with theism and, at least to some extent, with Christian religious orthodoxy. But the dialectical method, with its capacity for critically pointing to the inadequacies of any established argument or institution, together with the obvious difficulty of squaring Hegel's conception of a Spirit that is immanent in the world and evolves through human history with traditional Christian views of a thoroughly transcendent God, made the argument of the Left more plausible to a majority of young German philosophers.

Between 1839 and 1841, Marx composed and completed his doctoral dissertation on the differences between the materialist philosophies of two ancient Greek thinkers, Epicurus and Democritus. He was then forced to abandon hopes of an academic career as a new, more repressive regime consolidated its power in Prussia by excluding as subversive anyone tainted with Hegelianism. Meanwhile, the debate among the Young Hegelians was beginning to shift from the terrain of religion to that of politics. Marx epitomized this shift.

Ludwig Feuerbach (1804–1872) had been a hero to the Young

Hegelians during the early years, as Marx's close collaborator, Friedrich Engels, indicates strongly in his work of 1886, "Ludwig Feuerbach and the End of Classical German Philosophy." In his *The Essence of Christianity* and *Provisional Theses for the Reform of Philosophy*, Feuerbach had argued that both despite and yet thanks to Hegel's system one could see that the true agent of history, the only existing being really capable of realizing the perfections once attributed to God or Spirit was the human being considered as a species. Thus the real essence of religious practice, when properly understood, was the worship of the best qualities of human "species being." God, then, is but an illusory projection of our own best possibilities onto an imagined Other object.

Some of Feuerbach's outlook and method were used by Marx in two of his earliest works, both left unfinished: a paragraph-by-paragraph critique of Hegel's *Philosophy of Right* (1843) and his famous *1844* (or *Paris*) *Manuscripts*. But already by that time, in a small published fragment of his critique of Hegel, Marx had decided that religion is, so to speak, a surface phenomenon that exists to alleviate human feelings of suffering and that will disappear when the root causes of that suffering have been eliminated. In the *1844 Manuscripts*, he finds important clues to these causes in the universal *alienation* of modern workers. Their alienation, Marx writes, is at least fourfold: from the products of their work, from the characteristic human activity of working productively, from each other individually, and from their species being.

In these same writings Marx projects a vision of a future possible socialist society in which alienation will have been overcome and a new era will begin that will make the past seem like prehistory. In the new society, he also indicates in writings of this period, the modern bureaucratic state as we know it, distant from and over above the people, will gradually "wither away," its present functions having been taken over by the society's members. Hence, the "armchair atheist" Feuerbachian call for a critique of religion must give way to a more activist critique of politics. This move from passive, contemplative theory to the sphere of practice or *praxis* is epitomized in Marx's *Eleventh Thesis on Feuerbach*, written in 1845 but only published by

Engels more than four decades later: "The philosophers have only *interpreted* the world, in various ways; the point, however, is to *change* it." This was later selected as the epitaph for Marx's tombstone.

Forced by a political persecution, orchestrated from Prussia, eventually to emigrate to London, Marx there accepted the invitation of a nascent coalition of revolutionary workers' groups to cooperate with Engels in drawing up *The Manifesto of the Communist Party*, published in early 1848. This tract, written in popular language and in a spirit of international solidarity, encapsulates within a few pages most of Marx's central insights into the configuration of world history. It also contains detailed analyses of other socialist movements of the time. Its key concept, expressed at the outset, is that all past history has been characterized by class struggle, with one or another class at different times having the upper hand and then being overthrown by the class over which it had been exercising dominance.

The present era is seen to be a particularly crucial turning point in history inasmuch as, at one and the same time, capitalism has unleashed material resources and potentialities hitherto undreamed of and yet has generated a bipolar class opposition, bourgeoisie versus proletariat, more extreme than any previous one. The fact that the proletariat as a class is defined as having no possessions and hence no special interests of its own suggests that its eventual triumph over the now-dominant bourgeoisie would for the first time make possible a classless society. (There would be no new subordinate class.)

The rhetoric of the *Manifesto* is that of a call to arms, to revolution. This impression was no doubt reinforced by the somewhat coincidental fact that a series of revolutions swept large parts of Europe in the months immediately following its multilingual publication. But in fact the section of it dealing with specific proposals calls only for ten reforms—some drastic (abolition of landed property and of inheritance rights) and some quite modest (a graduated income tax and free public education for all children) from our perspective nearly a century and a half later. These proposals are said only to be "pretty generally applicable" to "the most advanced countries." On the whole, Marx was quite reluctant, especially when writing his more strictly theoretical works, to appear to dictate any future course of events. This is because he saw future society after the abolition of the capitalist order as open to determinations freely chosen by its members, the "associated producers."

This attitude becomes clear from a reading of his lengthy classic, *Capital*, of which only the first volume (1868) was completed before his death. (Engels edited the rest from notes and sections.) On the one hand, Marx had a grand vision of the overall course of future history, which he was personally persuaded would progress fairly rapidly along the lines imagined. On the other hand, *Capital*, which is conceived as a "critique" or internal critical analysis of the capitalist system with a view to disclosing its major practical contradictions in a dialectical fashion, seldom alludes to that vision and is always quite brief when it does so. Moreover, Marx's careful examination of the complex interplay of the capitalist system's components—the "exploitation of labor" (capable of being symbolically expressed[3]), the systemwide pressure for capital to accumulate, the occurrence of periodic crises of overproduction, and so on—yields no predictions of allegedly certain outcomes within limited periods of time. A prediction of a "certain" outcome at the end of an indefinitely long period of time is in effect not a prediction.

Rather, to cite a crucial instance, Marx offers an explanation of the phenomenon, noted by many economists in the nineteenth century, of "the tendency of the rate of profit to decline." But his analysis utilizes enough variables and "countervailing tendencies" to allow for the theoretical possibility of a suspension or even "temporary" reversal of this tendency, although Marx personally did not expect this to occur. Therefore, what came to be called the orthodox interpretation of Marxism by Communist parties later on, which stressed the supposed historical inevitability of the onset of communism worldwide, may have reflected the *spirit* of Marx's peculiar variant of the common nineteenth-century belief in progress, but it was unfaithful to the letter of his theoretical texts.

In the ranks both of those impressed by and of those hostile to Marx's ideas there are to be found dissenters to the idea that he should be considered a philosopher at all, except perhaps in his early writings. A text written by Marx himself midway through his career, in which he speaks of turning his back on his philosophical past and turning to the critique of political economy, reinforces this viewpoint. However, the whole grand strategy of *Capital*, although detailed economic and historical analyses constitute the bulk of its content and understanding it is greatly abetted by some familiarity with the terminology and framework of the tradition of "bourgeois" economic theory initiated by Adam Smith, is fundamentally that of a philosophical critique.

Among Marx's key philosophical notions, all indispensable for understanding *Capital* and none purely economic in a strict sense, are the following. First, there is the dialectical method, which he admits to retaining from Hegel while purging it of such "mystical" notions as Spirit that Hegel had emphasized. Then there is the deeply ethical lament that labor, which at its best is the expression of a human being's life and character, has come to be treated as a mere commodity. Indeed, commodities themselves have become "fetishized," replacing earlier religious fetishes in the importance publicly accorded to them and in their dominance over people's lives. Finally, there is the basic distinction between the *appearance* of fair, free, and equal exchange that pervades everyday life in capitalist society in what Marx denominates the "sphere of circulation," on the one hand, and the exploitative "sphere of production" that is capitalism's deep-structure "essence," on the other.

The truth of the matter is that Marx's way of approaching the enterprise of social philosophy departs radically in style not only from its immediate predecessor, Hegelian idealism, but also from the basic canons of the entire previous tradition. It does this by eliminating assumed boundary lines between what philosophy may and may not consider. Economics, history, reports of British parliamentary inquiries into dreadful abuses of workers and consumers—all are grist for his mill. Marx even, as we have seen, espoused overcoming the boundary line between theory and practice.

An important by-product of Marx's insistence on locating dialectical movement in human beings and groups considered as material entities, rather than in some alleged Spirit, is his critique of ideology. Since he believed that all thought is ultimately based upon and related to the material conditions of its time, however much some thinkers may attempt to conceal or deny this, he wanted to expose as illusory all "ideological" systems of thought, including most past religion, philosophy, and political theory. Such systems *claim* to be self-standing, autonomous with respect to the place and time of their elaboration, but in fact they are not. Marx's critique of "the German ideology," which he saw as culminating in Hegel's claim to Absolute Knowledge, is in reality greatly indebted to that other aspect of Hegel's thought framework that insists on locating itself squarely within its own time to the point of refusing to say anything about the future. By virtue of his critique of ideology, Marx is more responsible than any other single philosopher for the deep suspicion of all allegedly well-founded universal philosophical claims that characterizes so many contemporary movements.

Perhaps the most serious rival claimant to Marx for this historical responsibility is another German, Friedrich Nietzsche (1844–1900). Nietzsche wrote very little that could be called sociopolitical philosophy. Indeed, there is good reason to wonder whether a group of those imagined great individuals of the future whom Nietzsche heralded and called by the name *Übermensch* (superman or overman), could ever live together in a society.

It is true that one of those whom commentators have come to regard as an important intellectual forerunner of Nietzsche is the radically individualist anarchist social philosopher Max Stirner (1806–1856), whom Marx had mercilessly lampooned. It is also true that Nietzsche's work, much of it very unorthodox in style, contains some pointed aphorisms directed against socialists in general, without regard to distinctions among different socialist tendencies. He regarded them as symptomatic of the nineteenth-century tendency toward the decadent exaltation of mediocrity and leveling that had brought European civilization to the brink of a severe crisis of nihilism. Finally, it is a matter of historical record that Hitler later appropriated Nietzsche's name and thought, though in a thoroughly dishonest fashion, to give a facade of intellectual respectability to Nazism. But none of these or similar isolated facts amounts to asserting that Nietzsche himself had a social and political philosophy.

Nietzsche's writings are, however, a most important component in the process of putting into the sharpest possible question the idea, so central to mainstream Western social and political thought from Plato and Aristotle onward, that values are objectively real. Elements in this process can be discerned at many points in the earlier history that I have sketched, most notably in Machiavelli, whom Nietzsche respected, and in the historical relativisms of Hegel, whom he despised, and of Marx. But Nietzsche's critique is more radical. He advocates, as the title of one of his books would have it, a world "beyond good and evil," in which applying black-and-white moralistic categories to human behaviors and institutions would no longer be thought to make sense. Nietzsche thus appears as a forceful advocate of complete openness and creativity, and his message continues to have important ramifications for social thought. When viewed in this light, it should be obvious why his philosophy simply cannot legitimately be converted into some new, alternative political theory, much less a National Socialist one.

We have reached our own century, and the stage is set for the discussions of issues in a contemporary perspective that will occupy the remainder of this book. At this historical juncture, we find Nietzsche's advocacy of openness combined with Marx's vision of overcoming the ancient theory/practice divide in the otherwise quite different thought of the best-known American philosopher, John Dewey (1859–1952). Dewey's "pragmatism," as his worldview came to be called, approaches social and political questions in the same open, tentative, trial-and-error spirit as is to be found in the experimental method of modern science at its most characteristic. To Dewey, this was identical with the spirit of political democracy; hence the elitist, antidemocratic element of Nietzsche's philosophy was totally foreign to him.

Moreover, Deweyan pragmatism depends for its plausibility on the assumption that human beings are genuinely free to act, and so the deterministic elements in Marx and especially in later Soviet Marxism were unacceptable to him. Nevertheless, his curiosity and his activism led him to take an interest in and even to visit for himself the vast actual social "experiment" that Russia and the other Soviet republics became after the October 1917 Revolution. His gradual disillusionment with this experiment achieved completion in the aftermath of the official inquiry that he chaired, in Mexico in 1937, into the assassination by Stalinist agents of the erstwhile Bolshevik leader and rival to Stalin, Leon Trotsky.

This true story of treachery and intellectual disillusionment can serve as a parable for much of twentieth-century social and political philosophy, as indeed of life in general in the epoch leading up to the present. There was, for instance, a rather curious and rich revival of Hegelian idealism in a peculiarly British form at the end of the nineteenth and the beginning of the twentieth centuries. F. H. Bradley (1846–1924), T. H. Green (1836–1882), and Bernard Bosanquet (1848–1932) are the three names most closely associated with it, and the latter two wrote significant sociopolitical treatises. But the long, brutal, devastating World War, triggered by nation-state rivalries so intense as to override even the supposed internationalism of European socialist leaders, effectively destroyed the intellectual atmosphere in which such thinking could find widespread acceptance. In short, the long-entrenched belief in progress within what was once quaintly referred to as "the moral sciences," as distinguished from technological progress, was rapidly losing ground.

This process reached its logical outcome in Great Britain during a period following the Second World War that has been called, in retrospect, "the heyday of Weldonism." T. D. Weldon (1896–1958), now largely forgotten, was the chief proponent among social and political philosophers of a position known as noncognitivism. According to this view, words of normative appraisal, such as good, are literally devoid of all meaning content. (Their only content is said to be emotive, like cheers or boos at a sports contest.) Noncognitivism's intellectual affinities with Nietzschean thought are evident, although Weldon, who had participated in planning Royal Air Force raids on Germany during the war, might have objected to this comparison. At any rate, the reign of noncognitivism was taken by many to imply that social and political philosophy, at least in anything like its traditional form of theory-building concerning sociopolitical aspects of the human world, was an illegitimate and intellectually disreputable enterprise, since normative claims and controversies have always been central ingredients in it.

The Weldon period is by now long past in Britain, the Commonwealth countries, and the United States, and we have witnessed a considerable revival of social and political philosophy. In this revival, probably the single most frequently mentioned contemporary figure is John Rawls (b. 1921). I shall be referring to him and to other contemporaries in succeeding chapters. Meanwhile, Continental European thinking about politics and society took place largely in the shadow of Marx and Marxism until very recent times, when this state of affairs underwent a change almost, but not quite, as drastic as the corresponding political changes in Central and Eastern Europe. That is, although Marxism as such has fallen out of favor very widely, the Marxian intellectual legacy nevertheless endures and will continue to resurface.

The roll call of significant thinkers who have written in this shadow is long. It includes V. I. Lenin (1870–1924), intellectually second-rate but politically "world-historical"; Rosa Luxemburg (1870–1919), executed at the end of World War I; Georg Lukács (1885–1971), a Hungarian whose work has been the greatest single stimulus to so-called Western Marxism; Antonio Gramsci (1891–1937), an Italian Communist party organizer who was imprisoned by Mussolini; Walter Benjamin (1892–1940), Theodor Adorno (1903–1969), Herbert Marcuse (1898–1979), and other members of the "early Frankfurt School"; Ernst Bloch (1885–1977), an independent German Marxist whose work can be viewed as a sustained critique of the influential thought of Martin Heidegger; Jean-Paul Sartre (1905–1980) in his later years, when he wrote the *Critique of Dialectical Reason*; the collection of independent Yugoslavian thinkers known as "the *Praxis* group"; Jürgen Habermas (b. 1929), leader of the "Second Frankfurt School" of "critical theory"; and others.

For those readers who may be interested, I have attempted elsewhere to consider in more detail some of the comparatively recent currents in social and political philosophy.[4] But such current history cannot be our central concern here. Other, newer voices are clamoring to be heard, not only in the familiar "centers" of Europe and North America, but also on the "periphery" of those places that have for such a long time been defined as the centers: in Latin American, African, and Asian countries of the Third World.

What many of the new voices are demanding is, precisely, a "decentering"; that is, a re-examination of the many presuppositions about the nature of politics, of society, and of thought itself that have remained relatively undisturbed through all the vicissitudes of Euro-centric Western social theory. I think it very important that attention be paid to them, even while we remember and rehearse the history of which I have just summarized some of the highlights. For that history remains a very important part of all of us, of both our thinking and our institutions, even if we may not always be aware of it, and even if some of it may be painful and embarrassing. And so we shall proceed to consider some of the issues as they appear at the end of what our calendars designate, with an often overlooked irony, the second mil-lennium of the Christian Era.

RIGHTS AND FREEDOM

Given the lived experience of our contemporary society, it is appropriate to begin this discussion of issues in social and political philosophy today with the related topics of rights and freedom. By "*our* contemporary society," I do not mean just American or Western society. Concern with these topics is truly global, as recent dramatic events in China, the Near East, Eastern Europe, Africa, and Latin America have confirmed. Meaningful philosophy must respond to this lived experience, by clarifying the terms that are being used, by forging practical visions based on such clarification, and by projecting possible future worlds that would be freer and more rights-respecting than our own.

To say this is to assume, of course, that freedom and respect for rights are very high values. In philosophy, however, no assumption is unquestionable. In fact, as we have already seen, this particular assumption has by no means always enjoyed favor in Western thought. For Plato and Aristotle, for example, "freedom" had a considerably lesser value than did the virtues (wisdom, justice, and the like), and indeed they took democracy's emphasis on freedom as evidence of its inferiority as a form of government. Hobbes saw liberty of physical movement, which is compatible with a great deal of constraint, as the only legitimate meaning of the word liberty. He decried the bloodshed that had resulted from evoking some nebulous, supposedly grander notion of "freedom" as a slogan in the wars that had ravaged his early modern world.

As for "rights," I have noted that this word in the sense in which it is generally understood is of relatively recent origin. Ideas of legal claims that could be translated into our language of rights did, of course, exist in ancient times. For example, being a Roman citizen exempted one from certain punishments and other harsh treatment wherever one lived within the Roman Empire. Such exemption was, in the language of today, the citizen's "right." But whatever one now takes to be included among "human rights" was generally conceptualized differently, under the headings either of "natural law" or of the unwritten "law" of relations between tribes or peoples.

Jefferson wrote, and the Continental Congress approved, the claim in the Declaration of Independence "that all men are created equal; that they are endowed by their Creator with . . . inalienable rights; that among these are life, liberty, and the pursuit of happiness." He stated that governments are instituted to protect these rights and remain legitimate only by popular consent. However, these are exceedingly dogmatic assertions, admirable as one may consider the revolutionary cause. Like all dogmatic assertions, they are to be considered fair game for philosophical questioning. It may prove fruitful to use this brief text as the starting point of our analysis.

The Declaration begins, after all, by asserting that these claims are "self evident" truths. In fact, many thinkers have considered them not even to be truths, much less self-evident. Granted, the implication that there is a close connection between belief in fundamental human *equality* and belief in the existence of rights has a good historical basis. This is particularly true if we think of Hobbes' conception of universal, absolute rights among the totally equal but totally insecure inhabitants of his state of nature. Of course, given the pessimistic picture that Hobbes painted of this state, this is a comparison that the "Founding Fathers" would not have appreciated: it was not *that* sort of equality that they had in mind. Moreover, despite the traditional association of rights with human equality it is certainly logically possible also to maintain that different unequal classes of human beings have differing rights—some more or greater, some fewer or weaker. In any case, as we shall see, many rights advocates see no inconsistency in accepting both formal equality in the *possession* of rights by all human beings and actual inequality in the *enjoyment* of them by different classes, groups, and individuals.

Let us consider some further problematic aspects of the famous Declaration text. The implication that God's creative act is the source of rights is consonant with the views of Locke and of many other early modern thinkers. But it carries no weight with (a) nontheists, (b) theists (including believers in many non-Western religions) who do not think of God as Creator, and even (c) theists who believe in divine creation but think of rights as having some purely human basis. By the same token, with respect to the Declaration's list of three rights, there are many who question whether the "right to life" is indeed "inalienable." Is it really morally wrong to end life under *all* circumstances—for example, in the cases of fetuses, of pain-ridden hospital patients with no hope of recovery, or of murderers sentenced to execution? There are others who deny that "the pursuit of happiness" should be seen as a "right" at all. Is everyone obliged, as the notion of a right apparently implies, to respect equally everyone else's private pursuit of happiness wherever it may lead? Is this not too open-ended an idea to be considered a right? Finally, many regard all three of these asserted rights as hopelessly vague, the "right to liberty" above all. To be sure, the Declaration's list is presented as tentative and partial, as the words *among these* imply.

The Declaration further claims that the protection of rights is the purpose of government, that the powers of government are derived from the consent of the governed, and that a revolution against a government deemed no longer to be fulfilling that purpose is entirely justified. These claims would all meet with fierce opposition from some hostile quarter or other, as indeed they did. (The British of the time, in particular, were not at all keen about the last two.) Moreover, even within the Founders' own assumptions and worldview, deep inconsistencies and contradictions existed. First of all, recent feminist-inspired analysis has shown that there was at least an unconscious ambiguity with respect to women in the document's employment of the term *men*. Some maintain that the document actually meant men in the generic sense rather than just the masculine gender. But admittedly, none of the Founders really believed in *political* equality for both sexes. Others argue that *men* in the text should be understood to mean simply adult males. But the practical effect is more or less the same in either case.

Secondly, records from the Continental Congress show that these assertions about equality, rights, and freedom were not intended to apply to blacks or to American Indians. (This was true except perhaps in the more idealistic portion of Jefferson's mind, which must have been in perpetual conflict with another portion that sanctioned his being a slaveowner.) The assumption of inequality was stated in the most brutal and direct fashion some eighty years later by Chief Justice Roger Taney. Writing for the Supreme Court majority and on the basis of his interpretation of the historical record, he opined in *Dred Scott* v. *Sanford* et al. that "Negroes" (as blacks were called) "were at that time considered as a subordinate and inferior class of beings, who had been subjugated by the dominant race and, whether emancipated or not, yet remained subject to their authority, and had no rights or privileges but such as those who held the power and the Government might choose to grant them."

Finally, although upon a superficial reading the wording of the Jeffersonian text might make it seem that the alleged basic equality at least among the privileged group of white males entails that the listed rights are supposed to have equal force for all members of *that* group, this was clearly not the Founders' intent, either. Unless one is prepared stubbornly to maintain that "the pursuit of happiness" is really fully and equally open to everyone, regardless of the relative amount of material resources he (not she, since women have already been excluded from consideration) possesses, there remains a large gap between being equal to my fellow citizen in an abstract sense and being equally as able as he to "pursue happiness." It is unrealistic to say that the amount of money one possesses is completely irrelevant to how happy one is. Of course, some poorer people are happier than some wealthier ones. But the writer and signers of the Declaration of Independence were quite aware of this. They were certainly not advocating a "classless society" of a radically egalitarian sort. So the assertion of equality was not meant to suggest that any of the white males' rights, including their "right to liberty," should be of equal worth to all of them across the board.[1]

To point to the conceptual and practical ambiguities and inconsistencies surrounding formulations of human rights and freedom in one of history's most famous pro-rights and pro-freedom documents is not to deny its worth—much less its enormous impact, which is still being felt. But it is a useful reminder of the need for constant philosophical reappraisal of the meanings and value of the ideas conveyed by these grand words. Let us now leave the text and consider the concept of rights as such.

Do rights exist? If so, in what sense(s)? The answers to these questions obviously depend in part on stipulating the notion of "existence" that one has in mind. In other words, they depend on some ontological position, if only a very pedestrian, commonsensical one. In one very simple sense of "rights," lawyers generally have no difficulty in recognizing the existence of rights in any modern legal system. They include provisions for what an individual may expect by way of treatment and avoidance of abuse by officials of the system when he or she is accused of a crime, for example. A legal system is, among other things, a set of rules: Some rules are clearly rules about rights, if the word is to have any meaning at all.

A further question that needs always to be raised, even with respect to these most garden-variety rights, is whether they are *in fact* respected—that is, whether the rules are, on the whole, actually observed by the actors in a particular legal system: oneself, the officials, and others in one's society. This is always a matter of degree, of course, closely connected with important questions in legal philosophy about the existence of a legal system. But in any case I have thus far suggested two senses of the existence of rights: (1) the existence of certain rules on paper and (2) their observance in practice in a certain constituency. Taken together, these do not yet amount to a notion of rights about which anyone is likely to become very excited. Even an extreme noncognitivist like T. D. Weldon could admit that rights exist in these senses, as prescribed and effective rules of the legal "game," analogous to the rules of cricket.

There are many thinkers on the topic of rights who are not prepared to venture much beyond this point in admitting their existence. For there is a widespread feeling that any assertions about rights beyond those claims that can be directly linked to actual legal statutes written down in black and white (posited, to use an old Latinism), depend on unprovable "meta-physical" assumptions about the nature of human beings and of their social universe. It was in this spirit that Jeremy Bentham called rights "nonsense on stilts."[2] Some of the same spirit of skepticism about rights regarded as *moral* rules that are in some way implicit in *legal* statutes came to pervade legal positivism. This view took hold as an identifiable theoretical position in the work of John Austin, a follower of Bentham, in the early nineteenth century. Legal positivism contends that "law is law" and that the *concept* of law should be kept clearly separate from that of morality. That is, any alleged "natural laws" or "natural rights" that have not been specifically incorporated into the statutes of the legal system of one's place and time are by definition not parts of the law. As one might expect, however, various versions of legal positivism have developed. Many of them make concessions to antipositivists' charges that the extreme positivist approach is based on an untrue, unrealistically sharp division between statute law and the rest of reality.[3]

The simultaneous desire on the part of some thinkers to avoid making "ontological" commitments with respect to human rights (to avoid saying that rights actually "exist" in a strong sense as part of a moral world order) and yet to venture beyond the narrow limits assigned to rights talk by the strictest positivists is reinforced by certain unique features of the Anglo-American common-law tradition and particularly of the U.S. Constitution. Common law is based in part on precedent, which includes judicial decisions sometimes dating back centuries and themselves derived from principles that antedate written statutes. This makes a common-law system on the whole less clearly bounded, less tidy. The U.S. Constitution includes as its first ten amendments the so-called Bill of Rights. These have been among the most important bases of interpretation for the Supreme Court in dealing with vexing issues. The effect of this Bill of Rights, for which English law has no written equivalent, is to insert broad, somewhat open-ended, philosophically suggestive notions of rights, rather than just specific rights rules, into the American legal system itself.

The importance of these legal facts for social and political philosophy with respect to rights is considerable. In particular, Ronald Dworkin[4] is an influential contemporary academic lawyer and philosophical essayist who believes that an appeal to always-evolving notions of rights within both the American and the British traditions allows thinkers to claim that broad human rights exist as long-standing historical realities. This "compromise" position, as we may consider it, avoids needing to maintain that natural rights or natural laws exist in "human nature" as such. For Dworkin, the proper use of the term *rights* refers above all to "rights against the Government." These are protections against certain kinds of potential state intrusions in the free actions of individuals who are citizens of a particular country. Many of these rights, at least in the American tradition, can be and are designated "freedoms"—for example, freedom of speech and freedom of the press. But Dworkin rejects as much too broad the idea that there is a right to freedom as such. He points out that there are many morally neutral actions, such as driving the wrong way on a one-way street, that I neither am nor should be legally free to do and maintains that such laws would violate a general right to freedom if there were such a thing.

By this point we have arrived at a notion of the existence of rights that is considerably less narrow than the one with which we began but still does not claim existence for human rights as such, independent of particular politicolegal systems. Consequently, the specification of which particular rights there "are" is left relative to a given system. For many strong rights advocates, this is not enough: They want, like the author and ratifiers of the Declaration of Independence, to make more absolute claims. Is there any way left for them to do so other than to introduce some systematic philosophical notion of human beings in their environment?

There is one such way, although many proponents of a strong notion of human rights do not regard it as particularly promising: to refer to developing international practices and internationally accepted documents with respect to human rights over the past fifty years. Salient among these are the prosecution at Nürnberg of World War II Axis officials for "crimes against humanity"; the Universal

Declaration of Human Rights adopted by the United Nations General Assembly in 1948; the tendency in international law to begin to recognize that individuals and not just, as in the past, nation-states can sometimes have standing within it; and the frequent contemporary references, especially in Europe, to the Helsinki accords on human rights. These developments strike me as being serious and important. I believe that they point to an evolving world order in which the dispute between Kant and Hegel, reported in a previous chapter, is now in fact beginning to become outmoded. (The former, it will be recalled, had argued for the creation of a League of Nations as one aspect of a categorical imperative for world peace, while the latter retorted that this was unrealistic because international law existed *only* as an "ought-to-be.")

But today's political "realists" contend that Hegel remains fully correct, at least in this one aspect of his thought. As evidence they point above all to the continued lack of enforcement powers in international agencies. It is true that Soviet and Eastern European governments were riding roughshod over the asserted "rights" of many of their citizens even as they were ratifying the Helsinki accords. And the most recent U.S. administrations have, in effect, declared that they will abide by international declarations and tribunals, such as the World Court in The Hague, only when it suits them to do so. Thus, many say that it is pure equivocation to call international law "law" at all, and that by the same token internationally approved declarations of human rights have at best the value of pious but impotent exhortations to virtue. As for the Nürnberg trials, which some philosophers have even regarded as a practical vindication of natural law theory, cynics have depicted references made to the rights of humanity as mere ideological window-dressing for a historically familiar phenomenon, that of victor lording it over vanquished.

There is a further reason why even a segment of rights advocates refuse to regard these recent international practices and documents concerning human rights as legally binding. The Universal Declaration of Human Rights in particular identifies as "rights" certain human aspirations or claims that seem different in kind from the rights *against* governmental interference and interference by others that are found in the U.S. Constitution's Bill of Rights and similar documents. This new set of prescribed rights includes such items as the right *to* properly remunerated work, the right *to* adequate health care, and the right *to* adequate food and housing—in short, what have come to be called "subsistence rights." One disadvantage of the term *subsistence* is that it may suggest a minimalist approach, "the right to just enough to allow for survival." Some of those who advocate enforcing human rights along these lines consider this insufficient. But the harsher resistance to accepting the Universal Declaration as valid or binding comes from those who consider the broad notions of rights, of freedom, and indeed of the proper relationship between society at large and its political institutions that are implied by such an expanded list of rights to be ultimately incompatible with the more traditional view of rights as primarily "rights against the Government" and secondarily rights against interference from other individuals.

The United States government, for one, has not recognized the right to a job or the right to subsistence as a part of its legal code, nor is it likely to do so in the near future. If welfare assistance is provided by law, this is commonly regarded as a matter of practical necessity, not of right. In actual fact, private charity still furnishes considerable subsistence resources to the poor. This is enough to make it seem less essential, at least to the numerically predominant middle classes, to demand the recognition of subsistence as a right. On the other hand, our ever-growing crisis of a medical system that cannot be afforded by increasing numbers of individuals makes it likely that we shall hear more and more public discussion of the alleged right to adequate health care in the years to come. This discussion will obviously not be focused on the question of whether the Universal Declaration of Human Rights should be given the force of U.S. law, but rather on whether certain rights that happen to be declared in that document to exist really do exist or should be acknowledged to exist.

In short, regardless of the existence and/or legal status of nationally and internationally approved documents endorsing rights concepts both broad and narrow, it would seem that we cannot resolve the questions about the existence of rights and about what they are strictly by pointing to actual texts and practices. To try to do so would be to evade what is ultimately a *philosophical* issue. Are there, then, moral rights in a philosophical sense (that is, independent of particular institutions such as legal systems) and if so do they include subsistence rights? In analyzing and articulating responses to such questions as these, students of social and political philosophy can make considerable contributions to the ongoing policy debates.

Let us provisionally conceive of the philosophical notion of rights that is at issue here as some set of claims that all human beings are rationally justified in making to all of their contemporaries, either individually or through existing social and political institutions, and that their contemporaries are obliged to honor. These are claims to being treated in certain ways, including, when appropriate, the "treatment" of being left alone. This formula avoids, among other things, a possible initial suspicion about the existence of moral rights based on the fact that they are not observably describable parts of human beings in a way somehow analogous to physical parts. It is clear that rights can only be ascribed or imputed, not described as if routinely found by mere observation.

But there is another, more serious basis for suspicions about rights claims. It has to do with the uses to which they have so frequently been put in support of positions of dominance held by those asserting them. We should recall that in earlier times, before thinkers began more commonly to connect the notion of "rights" with that of universal human equality, it was the aristocracy that most frequently claimed special rights for itself—the droit du seigneur. But today the claim to possess special rights, though generally *expressed* in universalistic language, is frequently heard from members of the aristocracies of wealth and power, particularly with respect to property rights. Jean-Paul Sartre, in both literary and theoretical genres, has been especially adept at depicting the tendency on the part of privileged persons in twentieth-century society to wrap themselves, as it were, in the flag of their self-asserted "rights." For example, one of his short stories of the 1930s, "The Childhood of a Leader," describes the adolescent development of a wealthy young Frenchman of the period whose strong insistence on his privileged "rights" gradually leads him to become a violent participant in an anti-Semitic youth group.

Similarly, we find great skepticism about rights claims in some of the writings of Marx and of thinkers influenced by him. In exploring the grounds of his skepticism, we shall at the same time glimpse some of the grounds for the very different skepticism about alleged *subsistence* rights felt by classical liberals, who go by the label of political conservatives in the contemporary United States. This will take us to the core of some of the most fundamental arguments in contemporary social and political philosophy.

In an early essay "On the Jewish Question" (a critical review of a book by his former teacher, Bruno Bauer, concerning the granting of Prussian citizenship rights to Jews), Marx found problems with claims concerning two types of rights: universal human rights and citizenship rights. The distinction between these two types had already been made in the title of the historical successor document to the American Declaration of Independence, the French *Déclaration des Droits de l'Homme et du Citoyen*. "Citizenship rights" are, of course, relative to the particular state of which one happens to be a citizen; the idea corresponds roughly to that of statutorily guaranteed rights already discussed. Marx's concern here was that enthusiasm over specific citizenship rights (such as, the right to vote) may well blind one to larger and more overarching ways in which, despite and sometimes even by means of such rights, some citizens manage to mistreat others. For example, despite the existence of a right to vote, the dominant political parties may be manipulated and controlled by a comparatively small percentage of the population, thus leaving the average citizen powerless.

Marx's more sustained critique in this essay, however, had to do with allegedly universal human rights, our present concern. Marx noted the fact that this notion as currently understood only arose with the ending of feudalism and the development of the modern capitalist system. He believed that this put seriously into question the claim of universality. After all, he said, "universal" is usually thought to mean transtemporal as well as ubiquitous. He then singled out four specific such alleged universal rights, as mentioned in the French

Constitution of 1793, for analysis: security, equality, property, and liberty. What he proceeded to try to show in "On the Jewish Question," as he also did toward the end of his career in the *Critique of the Gotha Program*, and as many later writers influenced by him have done with respect to various formulations of "natural rights" within the broad liberal tradition, is that these rights concepts tend to be *interpreted* in such a way as to reinforce existing bourgeois power structures. This contention of Marx's needs to be taken quite seriously.

The "right to security" could and, by some today, would be interpreted as meaning a set of subsistence rights: a right to "social security," for example, in the sense intended by the name of the United States Social Security Administration. This interpretation would, as we have seen, disturb conservatives. But it can also mean, as Marx pointed out, a "right" to see that "law and order" are rigorously enforced by the police. In accordance with the latter interpretation, challenges to the existing distributions of goods and powers in a given particular society are strictly forbidden. This "right" then becomes merely a privilege of the wealthy and powerful in opposition to the poor and powerless. Moreover, human life itself is so structured as to be ineluctably *in*secure, terminating ultimately in death in 100 percent of cases observed up to now. This being so, what are the implications of asserting, as a universal truth about all human beings, that they have an absolute right to security? Is this not inconsistent?

The alleged "right to equality" is similarly ambiguous, as I have already shown in referring earlier to the text of the Declaration of Independence. Equality of *opportunity* for enjoyment, for example, means something quite different from equality of actual enjoyment. Every policy to promote equality of some sort or other entails compensating unequally for the inequalities of background and of personal endowments among human beings with which one must always begin. The attempted coercion of large social groups into absolute equality through a process of leveling, perhaps most dramatically exemplified in recent times by the horrendous practices of the Pol Pot regime in Cambodia, was characterized and soundly condemned elsewhere by Marx himself as "crude, egalitarian communism." What, then, *are* we to say this "right to equality" means? If we try to bypass the ambiguities of particular interpretations of the notion of a "right to equality" by taking it to a more abstract level, we may find it becoming contentless and empty.

The third *"droit de l'homme"* cited by Marx, the so-called "right to *property*," calls for special and more detailed attention, particularly in view of historical developments toward the end of the twentieth century. It is clear, first of all, that Marx was correct in pointing out that not every human society across time has *recognized* such a right, although those who make strong, ontological universal human rights claims need not take this historical fact as a refutation of their claims. Individuals or societies that have failed to recognize this right may simply have been confused. Plato, as we have seen, must be regarded as one such individual. While he did not write in the language of rights, he considered private property ownership as divisive and contrary to community values if practiced by the two ruling classes in his ideal Republic. He therefore disallowed it for them while permitting it to the much larger class of subjects, the ruled class, as a relatively innocuous practice for the latter to indulge in and one that suited their less virtuous and less wise characters.

Aristotle took strong issue with Plato's upper-class communism. Like Plato, however, he did not employ rights language in his defense of the naturalness of private property ownership. Property as a right, indeed the most fundamental of all social rights, for the protection of which government is said to exist, first came to occupy center stage in the philosophy of Locke. Thus he played a leading role in encouraging the connection that is now standardly made between the idea of a "right to property" and the rise of the bourgeois class and modern capitalism. Among Locke's successors, the critique of property ownership as "usurpation" (Rousseau in the *Discourse on the Origin of Inequality*) or even "theft" (Proudhon) should be considered in contrast to its systematic defense by Hegel. The latter regarded ownership as necessary, however variable the amount owned, to enable the human individual to acquire "substance" and become fully a person by being embodied in material objects. This brings us back to Marx, who saw the abolition of private ownership of the means of production and hence rejection of the idea of a "right to property" (other than, presumably, purely personal possessions) as being pivotal to radical historical change of the sort that he sought.

What makes this topic especially timely in the late twentieth century is the fact that regimes that had, in the name of their versions of Marxism, abolished or at least sharply limited the right to private property, most notably the governments of the component republics of the former USSR and its Eastern European neighbors, have almost universally and rather abruptly begun to reinstate and expand this right in response to widespread popular dissatisfaction with the perceived consequences of its previous curtailment. Of particular interest to us are the new perspectives that these changes have shed on the very concept of private property, the institution to which there is said to be a right.

In contrast to the notions of security, equality, and (as we shall see) freedom, property in the sense of *private* property or what is one's *own* is a comprehensible idea only when thought of as an institution, that is, a function of certain rules commonly agreed to. On this point, Rousseau's distinction between property and "mere" possession, a refinement and sharpening of an idea common to the social contract theorists, is very useful. The exact rules of property ownership, and the corresponding rights to it, will vary from one locale to another. In some they will be more absolute, with respect to individuals' use and enjoyment, than in others. But at least in the modern world they will never be unlimited, at least not for very long. The right to private property will not be permitted unlimited defense, for example, by owners who want to insist on conducting their businesses or industries without regard to pollution controls.

Even though property is not, then, an absolute right, it is often presented today as being nearly so. Among the most influential philosophers maintaining such a position is Robert Nozick, in his book entitled *Anarchy, State, and Utopia*.[5] Certain economic theorists such as Friedrich Hayek in the first half of this century and Milton Friedman in the second half have also affected many philosophers' thinking. Nozick traces the ancestry of his ideas to Locke.

Since Locke tried to ground the right to property in the "fact" that I "possess" my own body—a claim that, I think, is based on an equivocation about the notion of "possession"—he would no doubt have taken issue with my assertion in the previous paragraph that the notion of private property is comprehensible only as an institution, a set of agreed-upon rules.

Nozick's reinterpretation of Lockean social philosophy focuses on what Nozick calls "entitlements." These are essentially property rights that, unless originally acquired or later transferred through fraud or improper coercion, he holds must remain inviolable, or nearly so, for both the original owner (acquirer) and his or her heirs. This moral inviolability of entitlements is said by Nozick to obtain regardless of inequalities in amounts owned. The only justifiable qualification, other than some unspecified condition of tremendous catastrophe, is Locke's proviso, in his account of the basis of property rights, that there be "enough and as good left over" for potential future owners to appropriate. That is, no one should be allowed to obtain a monopoly over some basic good such as water.

Nozick insists that such a qualification, properly articulated, is really less a qualification than an understanding that is built into the very notion of the right to property. Whether or not we accept this, it is clear that Nozick and others with kindred ways of thinking, which were so popular among officials in the governments of Reagan and Bush in the United States and of Thatcher in Great Britain, are giving enormous scope to the right to property while endeavoring to anchor it in a broad philosophical worldview.

An equally important component of this worldview is the notion that a very high value is to be assigned to human freedom. Indeed, Nozick styles himself a "libertarian," someone to whom freedom is a supreme value. We thus come to the fourth of the alleged universal human rights about which, as I noted, the early Marx expressed such skepticism. To him, claims of there being a "right to liberty" sounded too much like a code that was being used to justify existing, highly unequal, property holdings. Of course the broad classical liberal tradition, from Locke through the American revolutionaries and John Stuart Mill up to its best-known recent proponents such as

Isaiah Berlin (the author of a famous essay, *Two Concepts of Liberty*[6]), have insisted that the most basic liberties are "negative" in nature. They concern freedom from interference by others (including especially a government) as long as one is doing no injury oneself.

But writers in this tradition have most often contended, or at least assumed, that having private property and a right thereto is a practical prerequisite, given the constant threat of coercion by others, for actually enjoying freedom of action. Many of these same writers are thus fearful of sanctioning any serious limitations beyond the "Lockean proviso" on the alleged right to property on the ground that this would threaten the right to freedom as well. They thus end up accepting the possibility of a world with great disparities of wealth and poverty.

Is not such a world one in which freedom is in fact greatly diminished and restricted for those who are poor—in which, in other words, freedom is by no means universally enjoyed? What concrete difference does the abstract assertion that everyone has a right to freedom from coercion make to a person who is disempowered by virtue of having virtually no material resources—whose "subsistence rights," if such things exist, have not been honored? These are the concerns of philosophers both in the Marxian tradition and in a number of other traditions, such as Sartrean existentialism, "Christian socialism," and "liberation philosophy." On such basic social issues, these philosophers share a range of views conventionally identified, at least in the West, as "leftist."[7]

Classical liberals are inclined to respond that critics of their account are in fact talking about a different, more derivative or secondary, notion of freedom, "positive" freedom or freedom as "self-development." This notion, the classical liberals observe, has all too often been used to justify a totalitarian organization of society that ultimately leaves no room for respecting the *basic* freedom from external coercion. This is precisely what happened in the Soviet experiment, they say. The elimination of class divisions was proclaimed as a long-range goal that would supposedly permit "freer" and fuller self-development of all segments of Soviet society and eventually of the rest of the world. But the authorities proceeded to

restrict or eliminate the fundamental right to freedom from interference, as well as, of course, the right to property, in the name of that
goal. Many who have lived under this and related regimes now say
much the same thing.

The critics, while not wishing to defend the often totalitarian,
dictatorial, and hypocritically self-serving aspects of Communist
regimes of recent memory (to say nothing of their economic ineffi-
ciency), argue that these historical aberrations should not blind us to
the conceptual inadequacy of limiting the alleged "right to liberty" to
the negative freedom from interference stressed by classical liberalism. Their point about not considering recent history as absolutely
decisive for settling theoretical issues is somewhat parallel to the
universal human rights advocates' previously noted dismissal of the
historical fact that in many past societies there was no recognition of
the existence of such rights.

No serious thinker today would try to argue, as Aristotle did, that
some should be free and some should be slaves. *Full* freedom for all to
lead lives that can realize full human potential, those on the left
contend, necessarily includes some of those elements that have been
identified with the "positive" rather than the "negative" concept of
liberty. Freedom of national self-determination[8] is one example of
such a positive element. Expanding positive liberty, however, would
undoubtedly entail encouraging and taking some actions which many
classical liberals would consider interference with individuals' negative freedom. For instance, affirmative actions to empower women
and members of minority groups are widely criticized for involving
such interference.

A simplistic reaction to the point-counterpoint that I have been
presenting might be to say that we have reached an impasse, such that
the "liberty" part of the alleged "right to liberty" simply means
different things to different thinkers and always will, and there is no
way of adjudicating between or among the different notions. But
other, more interesting reactions are also possible. One is to probe
further the stance of Marx himself, with whose skepticism over the
very existence of "rights" in the philosophical sense we began this
portion of our analysis. The notion of "rights," Marx maintained, is
subject to manipulation by the most powerful groups in society at the

expense of the others and is based on a fallacious view of human communities as consisting of atomistic, self-interested individuals. This justifies our abandoning it in favor of other approaches to social philosophy that would be more oriented toward the satisfaction of both individual and communal human *needs*.

Marx took this position while remaining a strong defender of freedom as a supreme value,[9] one that could not be fully realized, he thought, in bourgeois societies dominated by then-standard notions of rights, especially property rights. It does not seem too far-fetched, if ideas indeed sometimes have consequences in the political world, to attribute some of the most salient failures of the twentieth-century Communist movement to this Marxian attitude of dismissiveness toward rights claims. Marx did not, I am convinced, intend this outcome, but the inference remains a persuasive one.

On the other hand, we should always remember that philosophers' positions are inevitably shaped by the precise connotations that the terms, particularly the technical terms, of their language have for them at the time of their writing. Marx, in his critique of "universal human rights," was reacting to a certain widespread contemporary understanding of the meaning of this term that was at once absolutistic and yet designed to function as supporting language for certain particular interests, certain rising political and economic forces. This shaped his critique.[10] Faced with a different, more open-ended notion of rights, such as the provisional conception that I suggested earlier, his skepticism about the term would no doubt have been mitigated, and he himself might have been able to articulate his defense of freedom in rights language. He might even have been willing to defend "subsistence rights" against critics of the latter notion. In this spirit a writer influenced by the Marxian tradition, Carol Gould, in her recent book *Rethinking Democracy*, tries to answer the question "What Are the Human Rights?"[11] without assuming that hers or anyone else's is the last word on the subject.

Consistent with a more open-ended, less absolutist conception of rights, a number of contemporary philosophers tend to view rights as "prima facie" claims. In other words, they are to be honored by governments and by one's consociates unless and until a sufficiently strong reason is presented for overriding a particular right on a particular occasion in favor of some more important good. The suspension of rights in emergency situations, the occasional necessity of which even the most rights-oriented legal systems and social philosophies recognize, is an example of such overriding of prima facie rights. This prima facie approach, however, still does not completely resolve issues about the nature and extent of rights and of liberty that we have been considering, any more than does my suggested reinterpretation of Marx's critique of rights.

In fact, the appearance of an irresoluble impasse on this issue may be due in part to a certain traditional but questionable, dogmatic conception of social and political philosophy, according to the extreme version of which there is only one true worldview, and all other accounts must be seen as not only philosophically false but also politically dangerous. There are certain hints of this attitude in Plato's *Republic* and, even more, in his *Laws*, as well as in Hobbes' condemnation of the English universities for having spread "false" doctrines subversive of sovereignty. The most familiar modern example of this conception is the merging of philosophy and politics under the "party line" that dominated Stalinist regimes and for some years made it difficult to impossible to live a genuine philosophical life, which must include freedom of criticism, in them. Some time prior to the final demise of these regimes, the loosely connected collection of thinkers known as postmodernists began to point to possible connections between the totalistic aspirations of some philosophers and actual totalitarian regimes. Today, it is important to recognize that one can hear calls to replicate the same forced identification of philosophy with politics, but in inverse fashion, in the name of "the Market" and of classical notions of property rights, in many former Soviet-bloc countries.[12]

A less dogmatic, less absolutist, more open-ended way of doing social and political philosophy without wedding it to any particular regime is favorable to a sociopolitical climate in which the rights and freedom claims of a wide spectrum of individuals will be deeply respected. Every rational human being is to be heard in the ongoing dialogue. Different understandings of rights formulas (e.g., "the right to life") should be accorded respect, and no single institution— government, party, or church—much less any philosopher or other individual authority figure, is to be regarded as having the last word. No nameable concrete right, such as that of owning a handgun or any other specific kind of property, whether land or factory or bank, is to be considered so sacred as to be exempt from scrutiny and possible challenge and regulation. Only the abstract right of human freedom itself, understood to have many different simultaneous meanings of the sort that we have been considering here, is to be treated as unquestioned.

However, even the most enthusiastic proponents of philosophical and sociopolitical open-endedness in the name of a supreme right to freedom must in the end confront certain obvious difficulties and problems with it. Strong libertarians of the right, like Nozick, who start with a notion of property as fundamental to freedom of action, or of the left, like some contemporary writers influenced by Marx, who see privileged property rights as obstacles to universal human freedom, must both consider what a consistent implementation of their views would entail. For instance, should they allow unlimited drug use to those who wish it, or other types of behavior that, at least when practiced by enough people, would likely result in a breakdown of human community?

Practically speaking, material resources in our world are limited and often scarce, and to advocate freedom and open-endedness for all is of little help in determining how to allocate them. On a global scale, there is no consensus to deal with the enormous imbalances in resource shares between people in the wealthiest nations and those in the Third World. Moreover, past history in the form of ethnic, racial, and gender prejudices weighs heavily upon us in the world of everyday experience, and these reinforce great existing inequalities of power.

Advocating full freedom of self-development for everyone entails eliminating the processes of socialization that instill these prejudices from infancy on. But this seems practicable only if community structures are designed and redesigned with a view precisely to bringing this about. Merely waving the magic wand of freedom as an idea will not suffice. Recognizing that a social philosophy centered simply on rights and freedom would be an inadequate social philosophy, we now turn first to a consideration of justice, then to a consideration of community.

JUSTICE

The belief that *justice* names the highest ideal of social and political existence is of long standing. The past two decades of philosophy worldwide have seen an enormous resurgence of theorizing on this topic. The single most important stimulus for this resurgence has been John Rawls' book *A Theory of Justice*. The vast critical literature about it and about other new theories has raised many questions, not only about Rawls' own formulas and rival ones, but also about just what kinds of human concerns probably fall under the heading of "justice" and whether justice really is, as Rawls proclaimed, "the first virtue of social institutions."[1]

That claim is essentially identical with Plato's in the *Republic*, although Plato would have dissented both from Rawls' specific principles and from his principal overall concerns. A couple of the major areas of this dissent should be noted immediately. Plato's ideal society, it will be recalled, was to be predicated on the idea of everyone's performing the task for which he or she was most naturally suited. Much of the *Republic* concerns details about the education and lives of the imaginary society's small ruling group. Moreover, Plato showed greater fear of the undesirable consequences of encouraging freedom than he did an appreciation of its value. Rawls, on the contrary, seeks to *offset* the consequences (unequal talents) of what he calls "the natural lottery" in which everyone participates at birth. He pays comparatively little attention to the detailed working out of institutional arrangements once his two foundational principles have been chosen. He identifies one's right to the most equal extensive liberty compatible with a similar liberty for others as the first of those principles, a principle that is to be secured, whenever feasible, prior to the implementation of the second.

Rawls' strategy for establishing his principles is rather simple, though of course controversial. It relies on no strong overt ontological claims, although some critics maintain that it contains hidden ones. Suppose, he suggests, individuals representing several human generations were to be abstracted from actual space and time and required to choose principles for a real society, into which they would eventually be returned, that they could all agree to support as the most just possible. In this Original Position, as he calls it, they would be permitted knowledge of general facts about the world ("facts" of human psychology and economics, for instance[2]) but not of the specific place that any of them would be occupying back in real space and time. He calls this latter restriction "the veil of ignorance."

The stipulation that the parties in the original position must represent several generations is designed to guard against the possibility that individuals representing only themselves might otherwise choose principles that would permit the exhaustion of the society's material resources in a single lifetime. This is sometimes called, by others, the problem of "justice to future generations"; Rawls denominates his insistence on husbanding such scarce resources "the just savings principle." It is one way in which Rawls shows, despite his obvious aspiration to think about justice "sub specie aeternitatis" (from the perspective of eternity) as Plato did, his awareness of the relevance of certain facts about our own place and time in history. For the rapid destruction of resources in a massive and largely irrevocable fashion is a function of the vast new technical capacities of the twentieth century, which we have collectively employed so willfully to the detriment of posterity. On the other hand, his decision to conceptualize the problem of justice only within *single* societies and not "internationally," or globally, means that *A Theory of Justice* and much of the philosophical literature parasitic on it will simply neglect some of the most pressing issues of social and political philosophy in our time.

Through a back-and-forth process of considering various possible principles of justice and how their instantiations in real-world societies would actually work, Rawls claims that *his* principles would eventually command agreement among the imaginary occupants of the Original Position. He thus sees his theory as a more abstract, modern, almost science-fiction version of traditional social contract theory: All would agree to these principles, which could then be used as guides for constructing actual political institutions. He calls this method, as he employs it to persuade his readers to accept the account that he is giving over alternative accounts of justice, the method of "reflective equilibrium."

It should already be clear that Rawls does not expect his imaginary choosers to be highly altruistic, and that the distribution of resources, at least once the "liberty principle" of equal right to freedom has been ratified, is his principal preoccupation. Nevertheless, although he rejects classical philosophy's notion that the good for human beings is essentially a *single*, or univocal, ideal in favor of the assumption that we have a plurality of different conceptions of the good, Rawls denies that the denizens of his original position would be pure egoists, seeking only to maximize their particular, individual self-satisfactions. For, according to him, the *right*, as distinguished from the good, must be the object of *universal* agreement among the members of any society that hopes to flourish, and justice is the foremost component of "the right." In choosing their principles of justice, then, the parties would be seeking to found a society in which all of them could find satisfaction, regardless of any particular individual's final social status.

Rawls' preoccupation, dubious (as we shall see others arguing) in its exclusivity, with distribution of resources as the focal point of his theory is somewhat mitigated by his increasing concern with the Kantian concept of self-respect or self-esteem as an additional basic, nonmaterial good. However, his earlier list of what he calls the social primary goods focuses on four items in addition to rights and liberties: powers and opportunities, income and wealth. These are the objects of his second and more controversial principle of justice, which is designated as the "difference principle." He formulates it as follows:

Social and economic inequalities are to be arranged so that they are both:
  (a) to the greatest benefit of the least advantaged, consistent with the just savings principle, and
  (b) attached to offices and positions open to all under conditions of fair equality of opportunity.[3]

In effect, a just society for Rawls would almost certainly be an inegalitarian one, given the probability that a rigidly egalitarian society would not maximize anyone's prospects. But it would be one in which its least advantaged members would still be better off than in any conceivable alternative. He believes that the parties in the original position, being ignorant of their future status in the real world, would bet conservatively in favor of principles that would optimize their lots if they should turn out to be among the less favored. It seems obvious that a concrete instantiation of Rawlsian justice would, by virtue of the first principle, boast strong guarantees of liberty comparable to those found in the U.S. Bill of Rights. However, by virtue of the second principle, the "difference principle," it would be characterized by considerably smaller disparities or differences of wealth and poverty than exist in contemporary American society. Few if any of our social policymakers bother to reject new proposals as unacceptable simply because they are not demonstrably more advantageous for our *poorest* citizens than the alternatives. In most recent years, as statistics show, the comparative disadvantages of our least advantaged have been growing.

Disagreement with Rawls' theory has been widespread. From one side, let us call it the left, a variety of diverse criticisms have been made. For some of these critics, the central issue is Rawls' rejection of equality as the highest criterion for evaluating justice in distribution. Despite his initial insistence on equality of opportunity, they regard his acceptance of the likelihood of ultimate inequalities in power and wealth as an implicit sanctioning of capitalist values according to which entrepreneurs are the driving force of any society's success and deserve to be rewarded accordingly. Rawls himself would reply that it is not a matter of "rewarding" the better off on the basis of some "merit" of theirs. In fact, his strong plea against ratifying the effects of the "natural lottery," whereby accidents of unequal birth or talent determine society's "winners" and "losers," has drawn sharp attacks from some on the right. Nevertheless, it is true that his principles will not satisfy *strong* proponents of the notion that justice means above all equality.

Another frequent complaint from the same general quarter, to which Rawls himself has become more sensitive in later writings, is that he shows insufficient recognition of the likelihood that principles of justice may need to be made relative to historical circumstances, such as comparative scarcity of resources. True, he acknowledges at one point in *A Theory of Justice* that the normal expectation that the equal-liberty principle takes "lexical priority" over the difference principle may need to be suspended for very poor, undeveloped societies in which "the conditions of civilization" are insufficiently advanced.[4] But more radical critics maintain that historically determined differences in social structures—for example, the identity and relative status of different classes, genders, and other groupings considered socially relevant at a given time—do and should affect the very meaning of "justice" more profoundly than he admits in his book.

Finally, for many radical critics Rawls' initial emphasis on more or less quantifiable resources, such as wealth and power, mislocates what they believe should be more central criteria for a just society, such as the minimization of hierarchical relationships of dominance and subordination among its members. Rawls' defenders would no doubt reply that the issue of hierarchical relationships is in fact a question of power, or perhaps of a combination of power and self-esteem, both of which are on his final list of primary social goods. The opponents' reply is that their malaise runs deeper. They suggest that Rawls' paradigm of value in the domain of justice, as distinguished from the domain of individuals' private conceptions of the good, is *economic* value, and that this is a distortion of justice in the fullest sense.

Before Rawls, utilitarianism might reasonably have been regarded as the dominant approach within modern Anglo-American social ethics. Utilitarian critics, by contrast with those just considered, contend that Rawls' theory of justice is, in a sense, *insufficiently* quantitative. Rawls regarded himself as a utilitarian in earlier years, but he came to share the fear, already expressed by critics in Mill's time, that "the Greatest Happiness Principle" might on occasion condone doing grave injustices to a few individuals for the sake of this maximalist goal. Defenders of utilitarianism believe that the version of their theory that stresses the long-term consequences of adhering to certain rules and practices over the effects of single acts, now known as "rule utilitarianism," can accommodate these objections. Their approach to justice, they contend, can avoid the more complex, non-cost/benefit calculations of everyone's place or status in society that Rawls' theory entails.

But while this response may work in the classic case of proposing to execute an innocent alleged trouble-maker as a criminal, which is an issue in *retributive* justice, its applicability to Rawlsian questions of justice as *distribution* is less obvious. On Bentham's preliminary assumption, accepted implicitly or explicitly by most utilitarians since him, that each human individual is to count as one unit, the maximization of utility and the minimization of disutility in a society as a whole should not take account of anyone's comparative status or advantage of such. One's being greatly disadvantaged is a problem only to the extent to which it results in great unhappiness and disutility affecting the aggregate happiness or utility of the larger society. But Rawls believes that this way of looking at the matter overlooks the fundamental point of social justice, which is fairness to every individual regardless of the aggregate.

The best-known attack on Rawls from the right is that leveled by his Harvard colleague Robert Nozick, whose ideas we have already encountered in Chapter 5. Nozick's theory of justice requires perhaps the least amount of calculation of all. He contends that goods that have been acquired without fraud, whether directly or by transfer (including inheritance), are justly held, however large the imbalance between individual holdings (or entitlements) in a given society may turn out to be. As will be recalled, Nozick subjects this claim to only one qualification, "the Lockean proviso." This is a prohibition against acquiring a monopoly over certain kinds of goods, such as water, the lack of access to which would make others substantially worse off than before. In fact, Nozick attacks an entire conception of justice that is common to Rawls, to Plato and many other earlier philosophers, to the utilitarians, and to many strains of socialism. According to this perspective, what is to be sought is an allegedly ideal pattern of distribution, or "end state." Instead, Nozick views his preferred theory as an historical one, in the sense that the history of an item's original acquisition and later transfers should alone determine to whom it justly belongs. He thus regards even taxes, except those used for common defense, as constituting "forced labor," unjust and unwarranted coercion.

Faced with such a wide variety of incompatible contemporary answers to Plato's old question "What is justice?" the student may be inclined to think that the theory one chooses simply reduces to a matter of individual, personal conception, much as Rawls has claimed about diverse conceptions of "the good." After all, on the level of everyday life, there are those of us who are appalled that a Rockefeller or a Trump could at one time or another have had such disproportionately vast resources available to him, whereas others may find such individuals inspiring examples of entrepreneurship, at least as long as they prosper. Fundamentally and irreconcilably different views of what is "fair" and what is not appear to be at the root of such oppositional disagreements.

A number of strategies, all having some merit and points in common, are available to those who do not wish entirely to surrender the possibility of continued rational discussion about justice at this juncture. One is to point to the ideological nature of justice talk. Another is to rethink the meaning of "rationality" with respect to justice. Yet another is to concentrate on the critique of power and on the idea of empowerment. A fourth is to propose a fresh approach to the subject based on an acceptance of radical differences. Within all of these strategies (and there are doubtless still more) there seems to be a general desire to refocus discussions of justice away from the comparatively narrow issue of *distribution of goods* that has for the most part dominated recent debates—to refocus them, in short, on justice as a key or entrée to the further, broader question of human community.

It is to the Marxian tradition above all that we owe the critique of justice as ideology. An extensive recent literature exists on this topic. What Marx and his successors brought to light was the extent to which talk about justice, both among philosophers and in ordinary conversation, so often reflects, in an idealized form, an existing society's prevailing pattern of dominance and subordination among individuals and groups. Conceptions of justice in highly stratified societies such as feudal societies, for instance, emphasize the asymmetrical duties of serf to lord and lord to serf. These are confirmed and reinforced in theory by a comprehensive, hierarchical conception of a world order. Conceptions of justice in a capitalist society, on the other hand, emphasize the legal equality of both parties to contracts, including labor contracts. But they also sanction gross disparities in the parties' respective socioeconomic positions.

Does this mean that, for those in the Marxian tradition, "justice" must be viewed as entirely relative to a particular socioeconomic system? In that case, all legal, nonfraudulent transactions in a capitalist order, as long as they adhered to the *procedural* rules of the political system in which they took place, would be regarded as entirely just within that order. Some writers have argued for such an interpretation of Marx.[5] But it seems to me that Marx was more concerned about *substantive* issues, as we are here, than about important but secondary issues concerning *procedural* justice within specific political/legal systems. At the very least, it is clear that in Marxism we find reinforcement for enormous skepticism about both traditional and contemporary claims to being able to articulate a single truest and most adequate conception of justice to which all fairminded thinkers should subscribe, together with a theory of ideology to justify such skepticism. Some commentators have gone to the extreme of equating Marx's position with that of Thrasymachus, the view in Plato's *Republic* that justice is simply the interest of the stronger. This does not seem accurate to me, however.

Marx himself seldom wrote in the language of "justice" because, as is clear particularly from some remarks by Engels, they were both very keenly aware of the mystifying, propagandistic abuse to which such language is routinely put. On the other hand, it is clear that

Marx believed very strongly that some serious "injustices," or at least social *wrongs*, were endemic to the very structure of capitalism—however much his skepticism predisposed him to avoid speaking that language. Is it possible and consistent to take a radically critical stance towards "injustices" while refraining from formulating a detailed, systematic theory of justice in the manner of either Plato or Rawls? Either straightforwardly or at least in effect, numerous contemporary writers have asserted that it is.

Among the most influential contemporary Continental European writers is Jürgen Habermas. Widely read and very eclectic, he has borrowed elements from classical German philosophy, from current social science research, from Rawls, and from many other writers to forge a position loosely known as "critical theory." While this name is sometimes applied to other thinkers of either the first (before World War II) or second wave of the so-called Frankfurt School of philosophy, and is sometimes also applied to other contemporary social philosophers whose only connection with the city of Frankfurt may have been as tourists, it is traceable above all to Kant and Marx. Kant's contribution, as arguably the greatest philosopher of the Enlightenment, was thoroughly to *critique* the notion of human rationality. Marx, whom Habermas regards as being Kant's heir in many respects, concentrated his attention on socioeconomic structures while also frequently invoking the word *Kritik*.

Habermas builds on this Enlightenment tradition. One object of his criticism is the tendency, found in many Marxists as well as many of their opponents among economics-oriented theorists, to see all socially relevant action or *praxis* as determined by particular interests—either those of one's class or those of the profit-maximizing individual. If such claims were literally true, then there could be no common notion of justice, since by definition such interests are always in conflict. (The miraculous solution of a harmonizing "Invisible Hand" is ruled out as a mere myth.)

Another of Habermas' principal targets is the inclination, widespread in the contemporary world, to identify rationality as such with "technical rationality." This is understood to mean cost/benefit calculation of the most efficient means for achieving specific goals, such as a certain level of production of a certain type of commodity. But rationality is much broader than this, he points out. It includes the idea, which in the final analysis is an ideal of social justice, of everyone's pursuing her or his private interest in living a particular form of life that is satisfying for that person and *at the same time* employing our common theoretical interest in the advancement of knowledge in order to achieve our practical interest in a harmonious community. Habermas has considerable faith in the power of rationality, through speech or *communication*, to break through particularist prejudices and mystifications in order to achieve agreement on social objectives in the long run. He posits this ideal rational community of perspicuous communicators as his operative social and ethical norm.

Among the most common criticisms of Habermas is that, in constructing his magnificent ideal, he has remained too abstract and in particular relatively inattentive, at least within his theory, to the exercise of power and to the existence of conspicuously powerless groups, such as women. In fact, the criticism of Habermas aside, there has recently been a considerable resurgence of interest in power and empowerment across a wide spectrum of social and political philosophers. One source of this interest has been the work of the late French philosopher Michel Foucault (1926–1984). His analysis of the development of still-influential early-nineteenth-century notions about the efficient *control* of human beings—in prisons, in schools, and in workplaces—through techniques of punishment eventually led him into broader reflections on the social distribution of power. (Bentham had been one of the prime expositors of these notions, new for that time.) Whereas political science theorists of the mid-twentieth century (Arthur Bentley, Harold Lasswell, Robert Dahl, et al.) had shown very well how political and social power is actually exercised in a much more diffuse and subtle way than through governmental institutions alone, Foucault went well beyond them in demonstrating its virtual all-pervasiveness in human social interactions. He also had a somewhat better grasp than they of the sense in which power is essentially *relational*, rather than discreet and atomistic, a point well developed independently of Foucault by Thomas Wartenberg.[6]

Perhaps the central normative question raised by the recent focus on power is this: Is justice, or the suppression of injustice, better served by attacking power and attempting to minimize it to the greatest extent feasible or by seeking to give it to groups that have hitherto been unreasonably deprived of it? The answer, of course, depends on specifying the *type* of power to which one is referring. The term is notoriously polyvalent, multifarious in meaning. On the whole, contemporary writers on justice and power welcome the reduction and attempted elimination of relations of dominance and subordination. They distinguish such unjustifiable relations from exercises of authority over those not yet fully competent, such as young children, undertaken for the purpose of *transforming* the latter, when feasible, in the direction of becoming competent. This point is made very well for example, by Eléanor Kuykendall in reporting on a discussion by the French feminist writer Luce Irigaray on mothers' potential empowerment of their daughters.[7]

Empowerment is a key word, not only in contemporary French and American feminists' work on the suppression of injustice, but also among recent, primarily American, writers in the movement known as Critical Legal Studies.[8] They attempt to apply this notion especially to groups of poor people (such as tenant farmers) and oppressed minorities as well as to women. Racial, ethnic, and sexual forms of discrimination remain widespread and blatant areas of practices of injustice that are simply not fully comprehensible if we insist on focusing strictly on unjust distributions of goods, even though it is true that the victims of such discrimination are almost always victims of such unjust distributions *in addition*. Feminist legal theorists have pursued the understanding of nondistributional forms of discriminatory practice with special lucidity.[9] Similar in-depth systematic analyses have begun to be made concerning injustices of discrimination in everyday work or other social settings (schools, hospitals, the welfare system,[10] etc.) where the victims, disempowered because they are regarded as occupying inferior jobs or client positions in a bureaucracy, may or may not be women and/or members of minority groups as well.

Injustices toward groups may and sometimes do attain such depths of depravity, however, that to many they seem beyond the scope of Enlightened rationality, however broadly construed, even to grasp. In retrospect at least, and indeed to abolitionist writers and many others of the time, such may well be said concerning black slavery in the ante-bellum South, where some human beings received legal sanction for treating others as their property. A more recent case of injustice that to some thinkers is utterly beyond rational capacities to understand is the Jewish Holocaust. A powerful philosophical writer on this topic has been the French theorist Jean-François Lyotard, known as one of the leading representatives of the diffuse phenomenon called postmodernism. Lyotard draws, as one inference from the literally unspeakable event that is the Holocaust, a lesson of *extreme* skepticism about all thought systems that claim to be totally comprehensive—as Hegel's did, for example, For, Lyotard claims, such ultimately undemonstrable thought systems can be made to serve as justifications for *sociopolitical* systems that are totalitarian. He calls such suspect philosophical systems "grand narratives," as opposed to the "local narratives" that he considers it still acceptable for philosophers to recount.

Lyotard's skepticism about philosophical systems extends, consistently enough, to systems of allegedly universal justice. He contends that there is often a genuine *incommensurability* between rival conceptions of what would be the just resolution of any given dispute. In explicating this presumably pervasive situation, he uses an expression, *le différend*, that implies irreducible difference as opposed to difference that could eventually be adjudicated and somehow resolved within a single higher-level set of norms: "The title of this book [*The Differend*] suggests (through the generic value of the definite article) that a universal rule of judgment between heterogeneous genres [of discourse] is lacking in general."[11] If Lyotard's approach to justice is followed, we are indeed condemned to irreconcilability, and the Habermasian ideal speech situation is an idle dream.

But the potentially rich notion of difference, if not of *le différend*, can be mined to furnish a further perspective on justice with which I shall conclude this discussion. Rawlsian and other more or less "mainstream" theories about justice, including Habermas', have assumed the possibility of a point of view of *impartiality* from the standpoint of which conflicting justice claims could be adjudicated. Rawls' Original Position well illustrates this. What if this hoary assumption were misguided? What if philosophically relevant differences among groups of human beings were not only irreducible in terms of a single impartial standard (though not necessarily radically incommensurable in Lyotard's sense) but also morally desirable to maintain? Then the existence of many ethnic groups and cultures, of gender differences and different sexual preferences, would be something for a just set of social institutions to affirm and even to celebrate, rather than at worst to hierarchize in terms of what is the norm and what is deviant, or at best to neutralize in the name of an ideal of impartiality. An American feminist writer, Iris Young, has written a probing analysis of what such a "politics of difference" would amount to.[12] The intellectual atmosphere evoked by her theory of justice is dramatically different from that of Rawls' search for fair distributive criteria.

It is interesting that Rawls gave the key notion in his theory of justice the label "the difference principle." By means of this principle, as we have seen, he actually sought to minimize differences or disparities in the distribution of primary social goods among the individuals in his ideal society and to stress impartiality. One of the principal effects of a difference-based theory of justice, on the contrary, is to refocus the attention of students of justice away from what these newer theorists consider the excessive emphasis on the distributive aspects of justice and on the accompanying notion of impartiality that we found in Rawls, in his utilitarian critics, and in Nozick. Instead, a broader notion of justice as reciprocity affecting all dimensions of social interaction is being proposed.

But the mere respect for differences is not enough by itself. For among the salient differences among human beings in the real world are differences of belief and practice. These include many strong attitudes of intolerance toward certain other beliefs and practices and often toward members of groups other than one's own. It is to be understood and hoped that a true "politics of difference" will make a strong distinction between respecting, let us say, presently disfavored minorities and respecting the attitudes of racial or religious bigots or misogynists. But this hope does not by itself validate the first kind of respect while invalidating the second. Some additional theoretical orientation is needed to deal with this issue of whether to "tolerate intolerance," as it is sometimes called.

Thus, in making the case for reintroducing broader, not purely distributional considerations of justice, social theorists in the new vein that I have been describing are necessarily led to invoke additional dimensions of social philosophy. These have often remained only implicit in treatments of rights, freedom, and justice in early-twentieth-century mainstream Anglo-American thought. Such dimensions may be encapsulated in the idea of community, to which we shall now turn.

COMMUNITY

New discussions of justice, particularly of justice construed as distribution, continue to abound in the scholarly journals of social and political philosophy and theory. Yet a general feeling of dissatisfaction with channeling the discourse of our subject into such discussions appears to be growing. Systematic theories of justice on a Rawlsian model are widely, though of course by no means universally, viewed as excessively abstract. They fail, it is said, to furnish enough guidance, beyond platitudes, to cope with actual instances of injustice. These are observed, it does not matter whether directly or through news media, in everyday experience. For example: the vast misallocations and squanderings of resources on weaponry; the imbalances in the provision of food, of health care, of transportation, and of educational and cultural opportunities among different classes and other kinds of identifiable groups; and so on.

While it may be theoretically possible to expand the range of topics covered under the heading of "justice" to respond to this dissatisfaction (and numerous writers have tried to do so), there are good reasons for introducing a shift of perspective or vision at this point in our discussion. After all, the classical paradigm of a theory of justice, Plato's *Republic*, would never have had its enormous impact on Western thought if its principal focus had been simply Plato's definition of justice. This definition, it will be recalled, based on hierarchical assumptions about the distribution of talents and the division of labor, amounted to nothing more than the condition of everyone's performing his or her appropriate job. It is, rather, the detailed laying out of provisions for a supposedly *ideal community*, together with its underlying Platonic rationale, that makes the *Republic* so worthwhile even for those who reject most of its conclusions.

Community, then, is one name for the overarching concerns about society as a whole that an excessively narrow focus on justice, especially on distributive justice, appears to neglect. Another name, especially prominent in the Aristotelean and Scholastic traditions, is "common good."[1] However, suspicion of these notions abounds, and it comes from a variety of perspectives. Rawls, for instance, accepts a common modern Anglo-American philosophical distinction between two domains: "the Right," of which justice is a major part, and the Good, which for him must in an important sense remain relative to individuals. He shows reluctance to allocate more than a minimally necessary amount of resources to "public goods" and services, the economists' term for community enterprises such as parks, symphony orchestras, and state universities, unless the society's support for them is unanimous and they cannot be maintained by market mechanisms.[2] In general, current advocates of the privatization of resources are disinclined to endorse the idea of a common good that includes anything beyond the interacting forces of a "free market" and the government machinery to protect these forces from interference. Their "community" vision is that of a night-watchman state.

Marxists of a more rigid sort, on the other hand, see the notion of a common good as illusional, based on a failure to recognize the radically different interests held by opposing groups in class struggle. For them, the idea *might* make sense only in a possible future classless society. Critics from many other standpoints as well see in the insistence on community a threat to suppress differences and to oppress those who are different by insisting on uniformity. For those who nevertheless refused and/or were unable, because of gender, race, or similar factors, to conform, the only alternative would be exclusion from the life of the community. Fear of this implication explains, for instance, Iris Young's skepticism about the concept of community as she elaborates her feminist "politics of difference."

Nevertheless, social and political philosophers' interest in exploring and resurrecting the idea of community is probably stronger today than it has been for some time. Among the strands contributing to this are, in fact, certain elements of feminist thinking, which have the effect of identifying and criticizing the extreme individualism that underlies so much of modern sociopolitical ideology, organization, and everyday activity worldwide. Other strands come from the loosely connected set of approaches known as communitarianism. There is also a resurgence of interest in the broad tradition of utopian thought, of which the *Republic* can plausibly be considered the first great exemplar. Utopia, as we shall see, need not be equated with its literal meaning of "no place." With this equation set aside, we shall be able to explore, at least briefly, socialism and democracy as versions of utopian visions of ideal communities that are by no means necessarily mutually exclusive but rather interact with one another in many ways, at least on a conceptual level. Yet another such vision, anarchy, will also be introduced. Finally, we must consider a few of the serious challenges posed to sociopolitical community ideals from two different quarters—religion and ethnicity or regional nationalism—that emphasize alternative values.

Some of the recent impetus for rethinking community through feminist eyes stems from the writings of a psychologist, Carol Gilligan.[3] Her older colleague Lawrence Kohlberg had attempted, through longitudinal research on human subjects, to plot a general scheme for the evolution of moral thinking from the very young child's simple acceptance of parental commands to the mature adult's putative adherence above all to principles of justice autonomously derived. Of course, Kohlberg's developed justice ethic, somewhat influenced by Rawls' philosophy, involved reference to others. This represented, according to him, a much higher level of moral thinking than an ethic of pure egoism. Gilligan, however, was struck by the absence of female children from the original pool of Kohlberg's research subjects. She began to obtain quite different average results from young women than Kohlberg had from young men in response to hypothetical stories designed to elicit "higher-order" moral thinking.

Gilligan's suggestion was that women tend to be more influenced than men by what she called an ethic of *caring* as distinguished from an ethic of justice. (The story of "Heinz" that was key to the early research had to do with whether this man, lacking other obvious alternatives, should steal medicine for his very ill wife who needed it.) For present purposes we can set aside many of the philosophically interesting problems raised by this research. These include the implication, repudiated by Gilligan herself but drawn by others, that certain characteristic traits or attitudes are *essentially* "male" or "female"; the role of investigators' initial presuppositions in determining research outcomes; and the relationship between what most people at a given time and place *think* is moral and what may in fact *be* moral. Of greatest interest to us is the widespread renewed questioning, effected by Gilligan's influential and well-publicized work, of the supposedly primary role of justice among social virtues. Rules of justice have typically been claimed to be valid under all circumstances ("Let justice be done, though the heavens fall") except, perhaps, for situations of dire scarcity or other extreme emergencies. Caring, by contrast, is a less abstract, less formal, less rigid, more personal norm of behavior.

What counts as caring behavior depends on "careful" nuanced attention to the contextual details of any given situation: the needs, expectations, and state of mind of the care recipient, her or his particular set of values, age, gender, and so on. Implicit in the attitude of caring is a sense of interconnectedness with the objects of one's care; the self is viewed as an essentially *connected* self. Individual autonomy, a highly prized value within the very individualistic framework of classical liberal justice and rights theory, appears less attractive from this alternative perspective. For the person who places a higher value on his or her autonomy than on genuinely interpersonal relationships, cultivating a self-image that as far as possible excludes elements of dependence on others, reciprocal ties with other human beings are likely to be primarily formal in nature. A society of such individuals will almost by definition be an alienated society. That is, precisely, the condition of much of the modern world, according to a wide range of critics. To valorize caring, on the other hand, is to accentuate our sense of what the German philosopher Martin Heidegger called *Mitsein* (being-with)—that is, being together with others. This latter way of thinking thus evokes the idea of community at a very fundamental level.

Or does it not rather, more correctly, evoke the idea of *commu-*

nities? There are obvious practical limitations on the extent of personal involvement, of even the most diluted sort, that any one human being can have with others. This observation of course applies to everyone. One cannot really *care* for faceless masses. There is, then, an important sense in which the "feminine" value of caring and the idea of community with which I have tried to show its connection are unrealizable across an entire society, much less the entire globe. Yet there is another sense, which we explore in Chapter 8, in which it *may* be meaningful to speak even of a world community.

Feminist philosophers have been abetted by the practical experiences of many of them in helping to organize and work with community groups involved in caring activities—consciousness raising, support for battered wives, improving childcare options, and the like. They have been in the forefront of the contemporary turn to thinking about community. However, the new word *communitarianism*[4] has actually been applied primarily to the writings of a disparate collection of mostly male writers without any special feminist credentials. Among the most frequently mentioned names are those of Alisdair MacIntyre, Charles Taylor, and Michael Sandel. What they all share is a belief that the broadly liberal tradition that has dominated recent British and American social philosophy has, in both its descriptions of the present social world and its prescriptions (as in, for example, Rawls' or Nozick's theories) of supposed social ideals, exaggerated the importance of the isolated and abstractly conceived human individual. This has been done at the expense of individuals' interconnectedness with one another in community. In identifying themselves with past traditions—the notion of historical tradition across time is of considerable importance to communitarians—Taylor particularly invokes Hegel, while MacIntyre invokes Aristotle. But of course they also depart substantially from their respective intellectual ancestors.

Until roughly the late eighteenth century, MacIntyre claims, the very idea of "virtue" was, in Aristotle and in other philosophers and literary figures (such as Jane Austen), always rooted in a particular sociocultural community. Once this conceptual association began to be dissolved, he suggests, as it was particularly in the Enlightenment thought of David Hume, *virtue* became an abstract universal term.

The way was paved for the nihilistic deconstruction of the notion of virtue itself that is to be found in existentialist thinkers such as Nietzsche. This has created a crisis in values, he asserts, that can be overcome, if at all, only within small communities resistant to the barbarism of modern society. Similarly, the early medieval monastic communities served as islands of sanity in an earlier barbaric time.[5] In more recent work, MacIntyre assigns a greater possible redemptive role to the underlying philosophy of Augustinian/Thomistic Catholicism.[6]

Other communitarians tend to be less pessimistic than he about the chances for reviving a genuine spirit of community within advanced modern society. There are also "liberal communitarians," such as Will Kymlicka,[7] who protest that esteem for values of mutual assistance and common goals said by these critics to be missing from mainstream liberal social philosophy is in fact missing only from some deviant versions of it—in short, that the best of liberalism and communitarianism are reconcilable.

Communitarianism in all its versions points above all to a positive ideal: that of a form of social existence less alienated than the one that most of us live today, in which the society's members, whatever their individual differences, work cooperatively to achieve what Aristotle called "the good life." But how is such a life to be defined? Definitions vary from left to center to right along the political spectrum, and the very meanings of these different "locations" are subject to shifting, even to drastic shifting at times like the present. It seems to me certainly untrue to say, as some critics have, that communitarianism is an inherently *conservative* notion. Some communitarian visions, including elements (but not *all* elements) of MacIntyre's, are undoubtedly backward-looking toward some "good old days" or other in which there was allegedly a much greater sense of common purpose than is to be found today. But there are plenty of radically future-oriented communitarian visions to be found in the literature as well. For example, some, though not all, versions of communism (with a small *c*) advocate radically novel forms of human community. What does seem to be true across the board is that communitarianism of whatever sort implies some notion of utopia.

We need to reconsider the utopian tradition. No single contemporary writer stands out as exemplifying this old strand of Western social philosophy, of which Plato can again be seen as the originator, and for which Thomas More furnished the label. On the other hand, writers in the genre that has come to be called "dystopias" have abounded in the twentieth century. Such names as Zamiatin,[8] Orwell,[9] Huxley,[10] and Atwood[11] come to mind. This suggests that the concept of utopia, transvalued and transposed to fictional totalitarian horror states in which freedom and the human spirit itself are utterly oppressed, now suffers from an extremely bad press and is not a very congenial notion to thinkers in our century.

In fact, it is difficult to imagine continuing the enterprise of social philosophy without retaining some utopian element. What utopian thought does is to assert the role of the imagination in producing a concrete conception of community, or several alternative conceptions. Without some vision(s) of a possible future society proposed as superior to the one in which we now live, our bases for criticizing the present state of affairs would be at best inadequate. True, the utopian impulse easily finds expression in vapid, platitudinous, or sloganized forms as well as in proposals that are totally impractical. Nevertheless, the community ideals or ideal communities that it generates serve an indispensable function.[12]

Many historical utopian writings have tended to try to offer pictures of what Nozick has dismissed as "end states." These are supposedly perfect and complete societies from which any deviation could only be construed as a degeneration. Plato, for example, was quite explicit on this point. Not all utopian thinking, however, aspires to such rigidity, and the *Republic* itself fortunately fails in many ways to live up to the end state caricature. Utopias, certainly including the *Republic*, are in fact a mixture of underlying philosophical principles and of expressions of a writer's fertile imagination. They need not be rigidly bound blueprints. There can be open-ended utopias that lay down some of the *conditions* needed for a rich community life while leaving the community's evolution to that time, if it ever occurs, when such conditions begin actually to be implemented somewhere. Certain passages in Marx's early writings, for example, meet this description.

Indeed, much of the existing philosophical writing about community also does so. Such writing refers to possible common purposes, values, ideals that are capable of motivating commitment and allegiance. There is probably no need to point out the danger of intolerant fanaticism that can arise when some actual society's members begin to behave as if any such ideals, however attractive, were already realized and their society had therefore already achieved utopia. But a society without common community ideals, without *any* element of utopian thinking, is also at risk.

What can happen when widely held community ideals *dissipate* is no doubt illustrated by the current ongoing evolution of the former Soviet Union and other Eastern European countries since the dramatic changes that began to occur there during the late 1980s. A vague but meaningful ideal, historically traceable to Marx, had been proposed and begun to be implemented; let us call it "the building of socialism." From the early post-Revolutionary days onward, that ideal had originally been regarded as more than a mere slogan. But it was debased and dramatically *deviated*—to use Sartre's apt term[13]—by a threatened and doctrinaire leadership. It is no doubt true that many of the citizens never entertained any belief in the legitimacy of the stated ideal. Many others lost early beliefs as a result of one or another officially sanctioned atrocity. Meanwhile, however, it is also true that Soviet society, and at least some of the other societies brought into the Soviet orbit after World War II, at one time or another contained millions of believers or half-believers in the ideal. The East European regimes, long since eroded by deep cynicism concerning the leaders' own adherence to this ideal, collapsed one after another. As it appeared to many, there was an alternative ideal to take its place: the ideal of *democracy*. Its proponents discounted the troubling fact that the former East European regimes had also placed great stress on this same word, as in the name German Democratic Republic.

By surveying some of the conceptual and practical difficulties connected with attempting to articulate both of these ideals of socialism and democracy, we gain insight into major problems about the notion of community. These problems occupy center stage in contemporary social theory.

We must begin by insisting that many leading writers do not regard the two ideals as alternatives. These writers argue rather that the ideal form of community today would be one characterized as a *democratic socialism*. Mihailo Marković, along with others in the old Yugoslav *Praxis* group with which he was identified, articulated this notion for some years in various writings.[14] He often did so under threat of repression from his own supposedly democratic socialist government. Books by Frank Cunningham,[15] Carol Gould,[16] and Ernesto Laclau and Chantal Mouffe[17] are among others that deserve special mention in this context.

These and similar works include concrete proposals for constructing, through planning and legislation, communities that would exhibit much higher degrees of popular participation in self-governance than exist almost anywhere today. They would also favor a sense of common enterprise over the promotion of individual self-interest. These two components well capture and combine key insights from both ideals, democracy and socialism. But there is a potential difficulty. What if, as Cunningham asks himself at one point, a majority of the participants in a previously democratic socialist society were to vote democratically and decisively to discard whatever "socialist" elements inhered in their constitution? What if they adopted a strongly "free market"-oriented economy featuring total, or nearly total, privatization? Cunningham himself concludes that it would have to be accepted.

This, or something like this, is precisely what appears to have occurred in several of the states of Eastern Europe in very recent times. In addition to the complaint that earlier regimes in these countries had severely restricted freedom of expression and action, many of the advocates of radical reform there have revived the old notion of "civil society." This is advocated as a vehicle both for articulating what has been lacking in their community lives up to now and for bringing about the maximal possible restoration of private property ownership and "free market" commodity-exchange patterns. While the meaning of civil society in this contemporary context is somewhat vague and shifting by comparison with its quite clear-cut significance in either Locke's or Hegel's political philosophies, there is consensus that it refers in general to types of individual and small-group activities that were prohibited or at best inhibited in totalitarian state socialist regimes.

This renewed stress on civil society underscores one of the major criticisms leveled against much of communitarian thought across the ages. That is, as Aristotle remarked concerning Plato's *Republic*, it places the highest value on achieving unanimity instead of welcoming diversity or "pluralism." But Aristotle himself was a communitarian who accepted considerable diversity—as do, as we have seen, those contemporary communitarians who emphasize respect for differences. At the same time, Eastern European reformers and others have proposed the perspective of civil society as an *alternative* to socialism. But they must contend with democratic socialist thinkers who maintain, as many have consistently done since its origins, that Soviet "socialism" has been a highly aberrant form of what they have in mind, precisely because of its tendency to try to coerce unanimity. We must, in all honesty, conclude that "socialism" today simply means one or several of a whole family of ideas. These involve public control, whether centralized or decentralized, over major means of production; the absence of significant class divisions; the assurance of an acceptable minimum of major social services; and so on. But various advocates of socialism would no doubt *reject* various parts of this family of ideas.

The situation of the concept of democracy is really no clearer, despite the enormous hype it receives on world intellectual markets. Current disagreements about its meaning can, I think, be separated from the very different connotations that it had in classical times, particularly for Plato and Aristotle. In early modern times, especially in the context of the new American republic, discussion of democracy centered around such institutional arrangements as voting procedures and the establishment of separate branches of government to ensure the existence of "checks and balances" that would offset any extreme centralization of power. Indeed, during that period, "republicanism" was sometimes advocated in *opposition* to "democracy" as a way of indicating suspicion of too much direct political control by the people. Much more recently, especially during the occasionally euphoric 1960s when the utopian slogans of "Power to the imagination!" and "Power to the people!" were invoked, discussion tended to emphasize democracy of a direct, *participatory* sort.

Today, many of the advocates of "democracy" in, for example, Eastern Europe as well as in the United States insist on linking it with a free-enterprise economic system. They reject democratic socialism as a contradiction in terms. However, the converse of Cunningham's theoretical and practical dilemma about socialism confronts them concerning democracy: What if a democratically elected representative government, or even the members of a small community acting democratically in accordance with the familiar New England town-meeting model, decides decisively to institute "socialist" constraints or to control certain private free-market activities? This has been and is, of course, a frequent occurrence. It would be extremely paradoxical, at the least, to assert that such a development would make the community less democratic.

In fact, if we further analyze the currently fashionable equation of democracy with economic free enterprise, it is questionable whether a society in which free-market exchanges and other activities associated with the notion of civil society dominated to the exclusion of activities and institutions common to all citizens could qualify as a community at all, whether democratic or not. Lacking, in its most extreme version, any governmental institutions, it would by definition be anarchistic. Some "right libertarian" writers have admitted a preference for anarchy. But it would seem likely that, given an ideology of egoistic self-interest and in the absence of the restraints provided by a government, an anarchistic free-enterprise society would be pervaded by an atmosphere of fierce competition and mutual distrust. As in Hobbes' state of nature, everyone would feel a very strong need to be protected from incursions by his or her neighbors. The logic of such a state of affairs, as Nozick has attempted to demonstrate in his *Anarchy, State and Utopia*, would lead to the re-establishment of something like a government, though not necessarily a democratic one.

The alternative "left anarchist" tradition, on the other hand, as illustrated for instance in the nineteenth-century work of Peter

Kropotkin,[18] places a great deal of stress on the importance of strong community ties. The deeply ingrained human attitude of what Kropotkin calls mutual aid, which can be seen as an ancestor of contemporary notions of caring, could presumably under favorable conditions replace ideologies of self-interest. There would then be no need for privatization of property or for a separate institutional apparatus known as government. The question, dear to Rousseau and many other writers, of which form of political structure is "legitimate" would not arise; government as such would be illegitimate. This left-anarchist tradition involves, in Kropotkin's case, an appeal to the memory of ancient Slavic and other communities, some of which functioned prior to the existence of anything resembling governments in our usual sense of that word. Such communities could be called democratic, if the word in this context is taken to refer to a society characterized by close, nonhierarchical interpersonal relationships. But it is quite far removed from what most writers and politicians have in mind today when they advocate "building democracy" in Eastern Europe or in the so-called Third World.

There are thus extreme difficulties involved in defining the notions of socialism, democracy, and anarchy as considered with reference to community ideals, or, if one prefers, ideal communities. It has, I hope, also become evident that these ideals are by no means necessarily mutually exclusive, and that all three have significant utopian components. This discussion has at the same time pointed to the extreme difficulty and importance, in *any* social philosophy that stresses the idea of community, of resolving the question of which economic system or systems to sanction. There is no easy answer. The exchange of goods and services to satisfy human needs and desires is fundamental to any social life. In fact, an entity capable of being completely self-sufficient would not need to live in a society at all. But such an entity, as Aristotle remarked in defining the human being as a social and political animal, would by definition not be human. Without mutual agreement on some *system* of exchange, in other words some economic system, everyday human intercourse becomes impossible. It is therefore clear that any community-oriented social philosophy must address, as virtually all utopian writers do, the question of preferences among possible economic systems. The issue cannot be avoided, when we are dealing with ideals and not merely with what *is*, by pointing out, however correctly, that the system of capitalism is at present in the ascendancy virtually worldwide.

Moreover, the problem of economic systems is only one of several serious barriers to the realization of community values that must be confronted by communitarians of all stripes. In concluding this chapter, I shall briefly discuss two such barriers that we have not yet considered, although there are undoubtedly many more. The first is religious differences, the second ethnic diversity.

Contemporary literature on the subject in Western cultural circles does not usually emphasize this fact, but religious notions have never been far from the core of most thinking about social philosophy. Given the great diversity of world religions, it is notoriously difficult to specify what is meant by "religious notions." Let us tentatively understand them to mean beliefs in entities (Being, gods, One God, the Unlimited, and so on) and values that are transcendent to daily, mundane human activities. Thus the alleged inalienability of rights in the American Declaration of Independence was defended on the ground that they are God-given. The expansion of human freedom has been either advocated or opposed on the basis of its alleged conformity or nonconformity with God's will. Specific conceptions of justice have often been recommended as most closely resembling, within human limitations, God's justice. Plato's *Republic* ends with a religious myth, and many secular states of the twentieth century have followed certain ancient customs in attributing quasi-divine characteristics to their founders or rulers. In other words, they generate a substitute religion. A Soviet medal showing Lenin as a boy on the model of Christian medals of the Child Jesus was a typical illustration of this, as was the cult of Lenin's tomb.

Social philosophies advocating some ideal community concept must therefore deal with the question of religion, if only by advocating or at least envisaging its suppression, as Marx did. He thought, no doubt very naively, that it would automatically disappear as conditions of oppression receded. The worldwide resurgence of religious interest and even fervor in recent years would seem to imply that the simple *suppression* of religion in the foreseeable future is a utopian notion in the most negative sense of that word. But in that case social philosophers must face the fact that different religions, and indeed different branches or sects within the same general religious traditions, frequently espouse radically incompatible views and values. They begin with radically opposite conceptions of just how one's daily life ought to be affected by whatever one believes transcends it. For example, some may regard it as a supreme duty to participate in a Crusade or a *jihad*. When such incompatibilities are taken seriously enough by the individuals involved, the possibility of community vanishes altogether.

The predominant modern Western philosophical response to this dilemma has been, at least since Locke and the ensuing Enlightenment period, to advocate mutual tolerance in this area of social life and its partial or complete segregation from all other areas. Rousseau is, as always, an interesting exception. He sees his social contract community as one committed to a "tolerant" civic religious cult, devoid of all but a few simple doctrines such as the existence of God and immortality, but made a mandatory part of the community's life. Tolerance may work as a practical expedient in many cases, but it is by no means always so, and it is certainly not a satisfactory *conceptual* solution. Locke's own *Letter Concerning Toleration* excluded atheists and those whose religions entailed fealty to a foreign prince from the pale within which he thought toleration could or should be practiced.

On the whole, contemporary social philosophers have tended to avoid this issue. In part this is because so many of them remain heavily imbued with Enlightenment thinking. Habermas is an excellent example of this. But in part this is because the question deals with profound beliefs that resist ordinary garden varieties of reasonings and thus seems particularly recalcitrant to philosophical adjudication. MacIntyre's recent work, considered earlier in this chapter, is a partial exception to this general rule, as is a small portion of the recent literature concerning the legalization or outlawing of abortion. But this entire issue seems to me to be a blind spot that social philosophy can no longer continue to avoid.

The final barrier to community to which I wish to point is one to which most contemporary social philosophers have paid virtually no attention. But it has thrust itself into everyone's consciousness again as a result of developments especially in Eastern Europe, the former Soviet Union, and Africa: the barrier of ethnicity. It is not quite the same as, though it is related to, the issue of race, about which a great deal has been written. As Leonard Harris has shown in interesting ways, the notion of race (and hence of racism) built primarily on such physical features as skin color is far less clear-cut, far more of a construct with different definitions in different cultures, than is usually believed.[19] On the other hand, some ethnic differences that loom large in people's thinking are virtually or utterly imperceptible from the standpoint of any physical features, and sometimes even from the standpoint of language. (The case of the Serbs and Croats comes immediately to mind.) Nevertheless, they *do* sometimes loom so large as to provoke deep conflicts, hatreds, even unspeakable carnage. What motivates the parties in such cases are historical memories of distant and recent-past perceived injustices committed by one party against the other. This is the sense of "tradition" and of "difference" in its most virulent forms.

Such appeals to limited ethnic communities against wider notions of community are once again prominent features of the contemporary world. It may be countered that they had never ceased to be prominent. But that is not historically accurate as a universal generalization, although the explanations for reduced awarenesses of ethnicity in the still-recent past in some places where they are now re-emerging vary greatly. One of the tasks of social philosophy must be painstakingly to sort out the potentially positive, self-identity-building and community-strengthening aspects of ethnic differences. These must be distinguished from the devastatingly destructive effects to which awareness of them sometimes leads. In fact, the often-exaggerated and abused American metaphor of the melting pot reminds us that individuals of dual or multiple ethnic backgrounds abound in the contemporary world, certainly not just in North America. The historian will usually not have to go back many centuries in time to demonstrate, by reference to tribal and national migrations and intermarriages, that most groups' assertions of ethnic purity are fables.

Social philosophers have an obligation to combat the negative consequences of such illusions. Though they are frequently reinforced by appeals to religious differences, they are radically different in kind and conceptual status from the latter. This obligation, as I have termed it, stems not only from the perception that visions of ethnic purity are illusory and potential impassable barriers to community ideals in the modern world. It also stems from the fact that ethnic differences pale in importance against the background of the One World community. As the twenty-first century approaches, all human beings are increasingly being drawn into this as full members.

8

ONE WORLD AND THE FUTURE OF SOCIAL PHILOSOPHY

Near the beginning of this book, we saw the paradox in Aristotle's position in the history of social philosophy. He analyzed the essence and ideals of the Greek city-state, the independent *polis*, penetratingly. This was at the very time when its reality was yielding to the new world of Hellenistic federation under the leadership of the Macedonian royal family, with whom he had once lived. Though he was a good enough historian, Aristotle did not believe that history had much philosophical significance.

A similar phenomenon is to be observed among many of today's social philosophers. Their primary focus of attention has been the nation-state unit that has dominated world politics since the time of the Renaissance. It is tempting to justify continuing this focus by pointing to the already discussed recent revival of nationalisms in certain regions, notably Eastern Europe and the former Soviet Union. But this phenomenon is no proof against the easily defensible claim that a major historical "totalization" is currently taking place. The scattered revivals of regional nationalisms must be seen as explainable but, I have claimed, ultimately not dominant countercurrents. Social philosophers who wish to look to the future need to devote more attention to analyzing phenomena beyond the limits of the nation-state.

Totalization is a term borrowed from the late works of Sartre to suggest a conception of history as open-ended, in process, and not completely predictable by anyone. Nevertheless, it has an intelligibility and some general direction. Using the English words, he labels this direction as that of "One World." At first glance, this may seem to imply the idea that individual societies, and even history as a whole, can be viewed "from the outside," as more or less closed and structurally definable "totalities." Postmodern critics of such systematic social philosophies as Hegelianism and Marxism attribute this view to those philosophies and strongly reject it. But the two concepts *totalization* and *totality* are not the same. Sartre's loose notion can be used as a suggestive framework for developing a new, a more global social philosophy while avoiding the extreme implication of some versions of postmodernism that neither history nor politics nor societies are, in the last analysis, comprehensible.

We are surrounded by indications of our developing One World. To take just three examples, consider the worldwide standardization of credit-card usage or the fact that one can now dial directly from many, if not most, of the world's telephones to most others. There is a global pervasiveness of certain units (films, television series, music styles and hits) of popular culture, either American or at least in the English language. On the darker side, consider the sense in which a disaster initiated by human error in one locality, such as Chernobyl, can affect the well-being of individuals without respect to regional or national borders. Earlier parallels can be found for some of these phenomena. For example, French culture and language once had an international influence. But the scope and pervasiveness of the present globalization far exceed anything in the past.

The root causes of this phenomenon are in the final analysis largely technological, even though the mechanisms through which it has developed are primarily economic. Marx, when he wrote of the historical dependence of the "relations of production" on the "forces of production," saw this very well. True, he sometimes seemed to fail to grasp the possibility of historical exceptions to the general rule of technological "progress." Societies have for one nontechnological reason or another chosen *not* to pursue certain technologies as far as possible. Consider current limitations on nuclear weapons development and on maximum space exploration, for instance. But in the context of our present concerns Marxism's more serious limitations were its Eurocentrism and its facile assumption, inherited from the Enlightenment, that technological evolution necessarily entailed human social "progress."

To be sure, Marx was an internationalist, in the sense that he envisaged the socialist revolution as ultimately worldwide. But his analyses were necessarily rooted in the historical realities of his time. So he, like Hegel and so many social philosophers, treated single societies or nation-states as his focal point and the nation-states of Europe as their archetypes. As for "progress," Marx, the clear-headed, dialectical critic of the contradictory presuppositions and social practices of early capitalism, was its uncritical, undialectical cheerleader with respect to its destruction of all traditional values and its massive exploitation of the Earth.

There have, of course, been other global-minded thinkers among modern Western social philosophers. Kant, whose social thought has been receiving more attention recently, was an internationalist. Yet his ideal was one of a league of nation-states, and he did not grasp the rising importance of technology. Hans Kelsen, the legal positivist who dominated Continental European philosophy of law in the middle of the twentieth century, strongly endorsed a global ("monistic") perspective on legal systems over the perspective of individual national systems. Nevertheless, his concerns were deliberately confined to the single area of law, and he conceded that he could provide no conclusive rational justification for his "preference."[1] L. Jonathan Cohen wrote a small book, *Principles of World Citizenship*,[2] in support of internationalism as an ethical stance, using techniques of linguistic analytic philosophy. Wilfrid Desan has written a wide-ranging work entitled *The Planetary Man*[3] from a position informed by Continental phenomenology. However, a complete list of works of this general sort by European and North American social philosophers would not be long.

The list of so-called Third World writers who have attempted to look at our social world more globally, even while taking their own national and/or regional experiences as starting points, would be somewhat longer. Examples of such thinkers are Amilcar Cabral and Odera Oruka from Africa, Enrique Dussel and other "liberation" philosophers and theologians from Latin America, and the Indian postmodernist/feminist literary theorist and philosopher Gayatri Spivak. These writers generally do not think of their world(s) as third or even fourth, because this entire terminology has become outdated as a result of the collapse and/or radical transformation of the Communist regimes of Eastern Europe and the Soviet Union. (The latter were supposed to constitute the Second World.) One of the metaphors most frequently employed by these writers is that of center and periphery: Their native countries are peripheral. North America and the richer countries of Western Europe and of Asia, especially Japan, constitute the global center. Their constant plea is for a decentralization of both political power and culture, including philosophy. They argue for paying increased attention to African philosophy, to those aspects of Latin American culture that are distinctive, and to the special features and long heritage of Indian and other Asian thought.

Above all, these writers direct our attention to colonialism. This is to be understood first, of course, as a system of political domination under which most of Africa, much of Asia, and, earlier, Latin America and even North America existed. The political liberation of former colonies outside the Western Hemisphere took place for the most part after World War II; that is, within the memories of millions of those still alive. A few small overseas territorial possessions still exist. But secondly, and even more importantly for present purposes, colonialism should be understood as a system of socioeconomic dominance and subordination still very much in effect. For example, the dominance of most of Latin America by multinational, especially American-based, corporations is an inescapable fact. It is the large Western economic powers and Japan that dictate the terms for loans to these "colonial" countries by the International Monetary Fund and other financial institutions. To the extent to which the collapsed economies of Eastern Europe and the former Soviet Union out of desperate need have begun to forge similar relations of economic dependence, they, too, resemble the old "Third World" countries as colonies in this broader sense of the word.

The recent collapse of economic systems and ideologies may appear to create a condition of greater global pluralism, greater diversity, at one level. However, at another level this development has in fact increased the hegemony, the position of dominance, of the system of Western capitalism. While its proponents regard competition and hence diversity to be its foundation, this system nevertheless has a monolithic aspect in terms of certain common rules as well as in the form of gigantic corporations that preponderate within specific industries worldwide. A very important current development is the increasingly unified policy and practice of a large group of the wealthiest capitalist nations that calls itself the European Community. Meanwhile, the quantitatively measurable gap in economic resources between the wealthier and the poorer countries continues to increase. This is despite considerable hand-wringing by many thoughtful writers, some of whom see in this a problem of global injustice. Others are merely concerned about eventual widespread resentment leading to revolutions that might adversely affect their interests. Social philosophers of the "periphery" are constantly confronted with facts such as these, and they wish their concerns were more widely shared by their Western counterparts.

These observations suggest a possible strategy for bringing Western social philosophy into the third millennium A.D. It is possible to reconsider all the topics that have been featured in this book up to now—rights and freedom, justice, and community, including ideal versions—from a more global perspective. What is to follow is meant merely to suggest some lines of inquiry for future social philosophy based on scattered works already in existence. After briefly touching on rights and freedom, I shall organize most of the remainder of this chapter around the next of these previously discussed topics, justice. Or, rather, I shall emphasize its negative, injustice, as viewed from a global perspective. At the end, I shall return to the theme of community, but now from the standpoint of world community.

Rights, it is true, play a most important role in the conversations of social philosophy all over the world today, as already noted. A global perspective must take account, not only of individual rights, particularly the right to dissent, but also of the rights of entire peoples, especially national minorities, as well as of groups that have been the objects of special discrimination, such as women. In addition, writers imbued with a global vision and concerned with "peripheral" nations tend to emphasize that substantive economic rights, beginning with the right to at least a subsistence wage, must be regarded as prerequisites for the enjoyment of more traditional political and legal rights. When, for example, one suffers from chronic malnutrition and hence from a deficiency of physical and mental force, constitutional guarantees in a Bill of Rights become comparatively irrelevant.

Freedom, too, is discussed among writers concerned with what I call a global or One World perspective. As I have noted, there is a whole movement known as liberation philosophy, closely allied to the "liberation theology" developed some time ago by Christian (primarily Latin American Catholic) theologians interested in engaging in dialogue with Marxist thinkers and socialist ideas. The idea of freedom that liberation philosophers emphasize has much more affinity with the positive than with the negative liberty discussed earlier in this book. Since the memory of struggles for liberation from foreign rule is still very fresh in most of Africa, for example, African theorists may well think of "freedom" or "liberty" first of all in this context. On the other hand, it will be recalled that when Isaiah Berlin wrote *Two Concepts of Liberty*, he expressed doubt that this sense of liberation should be identified with social freedom.[4] Berlin had no intention of supporting the system of colonialism when he made this remark. He simply thought of freedom in a quite different way.

But like many other Western philosophers who see coercion as a generally unethical mode of human behavior, Berlin would have had less difficulty accepting the claim that the system of colonialism, the imperialist domination of a comparatively weak nation by a militarily strong one, contained many elements of *injustice*. True, colonialism was once defended by proimperialist writers such as Rudyard Kipling as a matter of *duty* on the part of the stronger toward the weaker— "the white man's burden," as he called it. Marx, too, wrote at length about the "progressive" aspects of British colonial rule in India. However, to give him his due, Marx was well aware of the brutality, oppression, and coercion involved in that rule to the extent to which it meant treating the colonized people as subhuman.

This general theme of coercion, of violence, may serve as a guide in considering the global injustices, transcending the borders of individual nation-states, that have begun to occupy the thinking of some social philosophers today and will do so more in the future. Three specific subthemes seem especially salient: war, ecological violence, and global economic imbalance.

The condemnation of warfare is of course not new in Western social thought. Plato, for example, while he considered wars inevitable, at least found the practice of enslaving prisoners of war undignified when practiced by Greeks against other Greeks. Grotius tried to lay down rules concerning practices acceptable in warfare. Kant argued for perpetual peace as a categorical imperative among nations. On the other hand, there was a general, almost universal, agreement until recently that wars are inescapable. And we often find a certain fascination with warfare's "positive aspects"—for example, that it offers opportunities for displaying the virtue of courage (in Aristotle) or that it brings out the transitoriness and finitude of human individuals and of individual nations (in Hegel). Moreover, beginning with the Scholastics, a considerable philosophical literature exists on the topic of "the *just* war." This is the attempt to define the circumstances under which it could be considered justifiable for one nation to wage war against another.

The idea of a "just war" has still not entirely lost its appeal. The popularity of a fairly recent book by Michael Walzer on the subject[5] illustrates this, as does some of the self-righteous rhetoric surrounding the Gulf War of 1991. Moreover, among American philosophers there has been a lively debate over the justifiability of the policy of "nuclear deterrence." This policy supported the build-up of arsenals of nuclear weapons as a threat. This is despite the realization that their actual use would have extremely negative effects, even on the country that first used them as well as on its foe.

But this debate shows that a major change is in fact taking place in social thought with respect to warfare, thanks in large measure to technological developments. As long as nuclear weapons exist, and indeed as long as the currently proliferating knowledge of how to make them is not lost, warfare has a global quality that goes far beyond what was implied by the old term *world war*. The latter simply meant that many nations were involved. But warfare under the threat of nuclear weapons entails an involvement of the *entire* world. This is true for warfare in general, not just warfare involving countries with nuclear arsenals. It is technically possible, apparently, for a terrorist group to acquire access to a single nuclear weapon and use it as a threat. In the troubles in Yugoslavia threats were made to bomb nuclear power plants and use them, in effect, as weapons. Warfare itself thus becomes a matter of global injustice, unjustifiable potential violence to everyone in our One World. It is no longer simply a matter of the relative justifiability of the policies of two or three hostile nations. A whole new philosophical outlook is required to deal with this.

From this perspective, it is possible to regard contemporary warfare as a special case of the more general phenomenon of ecological violence, the second of our three subthemes of global injustice. The ecological damage caused by the burning of oil wells in the Gulf War well illustrates this interconnection. The recent prominence of ecology movements is well known. They spring from a recognition, which became widespread only very recently, of the extent to which modern technology has made sometimes irreversible damage to the planet a real possibility. (In many respects, in fact, irreversible damage may already be a grim reality: the destruction of the ozone layer and the near-elimination of tropical rain forests are two likely examples.) Throughout most of the history of Western social philosophy, the predominant assumption was that nonhuman Nature, our planet, is justifiably exploitable by human beings to an indefinite extent. Now, few if any make that assumption any longer, and some social philosophers have begun to deal more systematically with ecological issues.

One of the important questions raised by the new global ecological consciousness is whether utilitarian thinking, which generally assumes that utilities for human beings are the only utilities that count, is adequate for coping with problems of ecological injustice. According to some critics, it may not be sufficient simply to enlarge the list of happiness-worthy human beings in such a way as to include future human generations, as defenders of utilitarianism against these charges of inadequacy have wished to do. It may make more sense to attribute some intrinsic value to the ecosystem itself, as well as to human beings. This suggestion comes from quite diverse quarters. For instance, it comes from the legal theorist Christopher Stone, who has suggested that natural entities, such as forests, could be given legal standing comparable to that of persons in the courts;[6] from Martin Heidegger, who argued for a certain reverence for the earth; from those who find the traditional thinking of Native American and African peoples, with their very non-Western attitudes toward nature, philosophically significant; and from some radical feminists ("eco-feminists") who find common ground between the modern feminist movement and renewed respect for Mother Earth.

If some of this new global thinking about ecological violence seems redolent of ancient approaches to the world that antedate all of what is considered mainstream Western philosophy and that frequently include mystical elements, this is not by accident. The formal conceptions of interpersonal, primarily distributive, justice which were discussed earlier are ill equipped to allow for the global, even cosmic, perspective on injustices that such phenomena as massive ecological violence now require us to consider. Glimpses of some such perspective are to be gotten from reading the other-worldly "Myth of Er" with which Plato rather mysteriously con-cluded the *Republic*, but the bulk of his and Aristotle's sociopolitical thinking was addressed to the question of justice within a single, mundane *polis*. Much of what followed them was similarly con-cerned with justice within a single *regnum* (kingdom, realm). The rise of the modern nation-state coincided with the development of a more rigorously and more narrowly defined conception of ratio-nality, characteristic of the Enlightenment, that took for granted the reasonableness and justice of exploiting Nature for human purposes. Hence the new thinking that is called for with respect to ecological violence may well need to borrow from pre-Enlightenment and even pre-classical thought as well as from contemporary wisdom. What is clear, at any rate, is that the problems of ecology will oblige any One World social philosophy of the future to develop a new ethic of caring. This can no longer just be on the level of caring within human communities or the human community, but must be on the level of caring for the Earth itself.

It remains true that the principal focus of social philosophy as such is human beings in society. It is the situation of extreme disparity of resources between different sectors of the world's current population that constitutes the third and final subtheme of global injustice I have proposed. Western social philosophers have always noted the disparities between the rich and the poor and have frequently, though not universally, warned against allowing them to become too great. What is different and new about such current discrepancies is their truly global scale and their more systematic nature. By the latter I mean that the socioeconomic mechanisms whereby they are maintained and even increased are more contrived and visible. They are less a matter of purely rational accident or of the simple fortunes of war than at any time in past history.

What is controversial about my characterization of the global imbalance of resources is to include it as an instance of violence or coercion. Some, perhaps many, philosophers would not even wish to regard it as an instance of *injustice*. Of course the facts of global economic dominance and subordination today are beyond dispute, almost all would agree. Certain identifiable nations are vastly wealthier than the rest and in large measure control the chances of the latter to improve their status. Thus they effectively create a veto power over their policies. But some would say that these are not injustices because not consciously willed by any one individual or group. *Certainly* they are not violent or coercive, it would be said, because they are not generally maintained by the active use of force.

I shall justify my classification of the global imbalance of resources as injustice and violence simply by saying that it is keenly felt as such by many residents of "peripheral" nations and philosophers who speak for them. It is they who suffer from a paucity of resources and have reason to envy the riches of their wealthy counterparts. They feel that the huge discrepancies in wealth have no basis in merit and that the past historical events that helped to create the present state of affairs were themselves often morally unjustifiable acts of great violence. The appropriation of the Americas by white colonizers is an obvious case in point. As for violence in the present, they know that any political leader with a program for large-scale redistribution of a valuable resource such as oil will at least be isolated and treated in an unfriendly manner by leaders of the wealthy "metropolitan" countries.

This is a point of view any social philosopher eager to develop a global perspective must confront. It is a more difficult issue to confront than those of war or ecology. On the nature of these there is more of a consensus at a certain level, although the philosophical frameworks for dealing with them may differ greatly. Yet the issue of the global imbalance of resources is central to any discussion of the nascent One World of the future.

Marx remarked at one point that the private possession of tracts of the Earth by single individuals will some day, from a higher social standpoint, appear as irrational as the ownership of some human beings by others, slavery, appears to us.[7] He wrote this at about the same time, less than a century and a half ago, as the American Civil War was just putting an end to widespread slavery in one of the world's supposedly less backward countries. Thus, even the irrationality of slavery must not have been universally obvious at that time. Marx's own thought is currently in eclipse as a result of the collapse of regimes that had claimed him as their inspiration. Moreover, the emphasis on physical land in this text, one of the few in *Capital* in which Marx discusses agriculture as an industry at length, is far from the locus of the greatest global wealth today. This locus is the intangible capital assets that he himself presciently identified as the central realities of the near future. Nevertheless, the underlying philosophical point of his statement is worth considering. It can be applied, for example, to the control of vast landholdings by a few families in agricultural Latin American countries, to the ownership of major shares in oil deposits by a handful of Middle Eastern rulers, and to the less directly perceivable possession of enormous global resources by the majority stockholders of some multinational corporations.

What is the rationality of the present distribution of the world's wealth? Is it that the nicest people have the most? Surely not, and surely not the reverse, either. Given the global fact of widespread malnutrition, as well as other effects of severe economic deprivation, is there not a moral obligation on the part of those with more than enough to "give of their abundance" to those who are deprived? In today's technologically advanced world, surely practical mechanisms for large-scale redistribution of resources exist. In particular crises, they have already been utilized: huge airdrops of food, to take a very simple example. That there should be no effort at redistribution at all, not even at times of major crises such as famines, is not a popular point of view in the existing literature on this topic, but there is little agreement beyond that. The philosophical task for the future, then, is to determine to what extent the redistribution mechanisms should be utilized, on what ground, and to what end.

Finally, the question of the end takes us back, at the global level, to the theme of community considered in the preceding chapter. What should, or will, the social philosophy of the future have to say about *world* community? We can at least say that it must feature more equitable resource distribution, more respect for the environment, and far fewer wars and threats of wars than our present world. But it will be important to avoid devising facile utopias about this future world. Much of the current "postmodern" resentment against talk of totalities is a reaction to some Marxian and other versions of global social utopias, or ideal world communities. Attempts to interpret and implement them have shown their extreme inadequacies when viewed as "blueprints." Marx, as already noted, had no intention of proposing a grand master plan for the future, but he is still widely regarded as having done so. Thus, as is frequent, if one takes "world community" to mean some sort of constitution for a world government and social order, social philosophers would do well to refrain from making any such proposed constitution their principal focus of attention.

It is all too easy, too, for philosophers to adopt as their own some partisan scheme, advanced by one or several current national governments, for organizing our increasingly One World along their preferred lines. Such was the nature of the Third and Fourth Internationals of the early and mid-twentieth century. Such, too, seemed to be the character of the new world order advocated by the American government during the Gulf War period. Philosophy always does best to remain primarily a *critical* discipline.

Future social philosophers can, however, draw ideas both from recent feminist and other literature mentioned in the preceding chapter and from the very strong and often quite non-Western conceptions of community to be found in works about philosophy from "peripheral" nations, particularly those of Africa in this case. The key notion, schematically put, is to combine a sense of reciprocal caring with a respect for differences of gender, of race, of ethnic, religious, and other historical traditions. If we do this, other features appropriate to the technological nature of the "postmodern" world can be added. In particular, our ability in principle drastically to reduce material scarcity for everyone in some key areas of life, such as nutrition, must be recognized and viewed against the continuing widespread existence of such scarcities. Only then can it be seen how far our world "community" falls short even of its present possibilities and hence how premature and inappropriate much of the cheering about human social progress has been.

But it is not only *material* scarcities, in the narrow sense, that must be considered in light of community ideals viewed from a global perspective. We must also acknowledge the atmosphere of intellectual or spiritual scarcity that results in the failure of so many to pose necessary philosophical questions about the One World toward which we are moving. Even some of the best of present mainstream work in social philosophy abets, or at least does not do enough to dissipate, this atmosphere. But social philosophy in the future should encourage both new questions and the hearing of new voices formerly considered peripheral from the standpoint of the Western tradition.

Recently, there have been some highly publicized attacks, from self-styled defenders of that tradition, on the efforts of certain universities to broaden their general curricula along nontraditional lines. Such attacks are particularly inappropriate when carried out in the name of our point of departure in this book: Classical Greek thought and especially the philosophy of Plato. For Plato traveled widely within his world and made use of the diverse wisdoms he absorbed from far beyond his native Attica. He was also a wise man who *knew* that there were many worlds of thought beyond his own contemporary world and realities that were inarticulable within the limitations of even the most sophisticated language and thought of his day. And in this he was right.

NOTES

Chapter One

1 "Antigone," in *Sophocles I/Three Tragedies*, ed. Grene and Lattimore, tr. E. Wyckoff (Chicago: University of Chicago Press, 1954), p. 174.

2 Thucydides, *The Peloponnesian War*, tr. J. H. Finley, Jr. (New York: Modern Library), p. 104.

3 Ibid., p. 113.

4 Ibid., p. 334.

5 Ibid., p. 337.

6 On this point I accept the judgment of my late teacher, A. P. d'Entrèves, who makes this claim on p. 25 of his *Natural Law*, 2nd ed. (London: Hutchinson, 1970). The passage in *De Re Publica*, which is a magnificent statement of the universalistic natural law ideal, is at III, xxiii, 33.

7 In *Capital*, Vol. I, Chap. XXIV, Sect. 3, tr. Moore and Aveling (Moscow: Foreign Languages Publishing House, 1961), pp. 592–593.

8 Thucydides, op. cit., p. 106.

Chapter Two

1 Thomas More, *Utopia*, tr. H. V. S. Ogden (New York: Appleton-Century Crofts, 1949), p. 9.

2 Thomas Hobbes, *Leviathan*, ed. Oakeshott (Oxford: Basil Blackwell, 1960), Chap. XIX, p. 121.

3 Ibid, Chap. *XXI*, p. 141.

4 John Locke, *Two Treatises of Government* (New York: Hafner Publishing, 1947), Second Treatise, Chap. IX, p. 184.

5 Ibid., Chap. II, p. 123.

[6] *Fundamental Constitutions of Carolina*, in *The Works of John Locke*, 12th ed. (London: C. Baldwin, 1829), Vol. 9, p. 196.

Chapter Three

[1] Rousseau, *Du Contrat Social* I, x. Author's translation.
[2] Ibid., II, vii. Author's translation.
[3] "[A crime] is a breach and violation of the public right and of duties due to the whole community considered as such, and in its social and aggregate capacity. . . ." From Brown, in *Black's Law Dictionary*, 4th ed. (St. Paul, Minn.: West Publishing Co., 1951), p. 445.

Chapter Four

[1] Burke, *Reflections on the Revolution in France* (Indianapolis, Ind.: Hackett, 1987), p. 66.
[2] Ibid., Vol. 1, Chap. VI, p. 176. There is also a later footnote that begins: "Bentham is a purely English phenomenon. . . . In no time and in no country has the most homespun commonplace ever strutted about in so self-satisfied a way." Vol. 1, Ch. XXIV, Section 5, p. 609.
[3] For Marx, the rate of exploitation is quantitatively measurable in principle. It is s/v. s represents surplus value, or the amount of time per calendar unit (day or week or year) spent by a worker in producing added value beyond what is needed to pay for his or her subsistence wage. v is variable capital, the employer's outlay, per calendar unit, for the wage.
[4] McBride, *Social Theory at a Crossroads* (Pittsburgh: Duquesne University Press, 1980).

Chapter Five

[1] John Rawls, in *A Theory of Justice* (Cambridge, Mass.: Harvard University Press, 1971), makes a sharp distinction between equal liberty, which is his first principle of justice, and the *worth* of liberty, which may admittedly be quite unequal for different individuals (p. 204).
[2] Cited in Ronald Dworkin, *Taking Rights Seriously* (Cambridge, Mass.: Harvard University Press, 1977), p. 184.
[3] H. L. A. Hart, a British philosopher and expert in jurisprudence, has sorted out some of these matters well in his seminal mid-twentieth-century work, *The Concept of Law* (Oxford: Clarendon Press, 1961). See, in particular, his footnote, p. 253, on the component elements of various versions of legal positivism; his own version of the "separation of law from morals" is less rigid than those of, for

instance, John Austin in the nineteenth century or Hans Kelsen in the early twentieth.

4 Dworkin, op cit.

5 Robert Nozick, *Anarchy, State, and Utopia* (New York: Basic Books, 1974).

6 Isaiah Berlin, *Two Concepts of Liberty* (Oxford: Clarendon Press, 1958). However, in the introduction to a later printing of his original essay, Berlin admitted that his ringing defense of "negative" as opposed to "positive" freedom should not be seen as presenting an absolute "either-or" choice. A society in which freedom from interference is honored is not incompatible with socialism, he acknowledged, and in fact there is an element of self-realization or self-fulfillment, an idea that he had originally identified with "positive" freedom, implicit in his assertion that negative freedom is valuable because it leaves room for more human possibilities. See his *Four Essays on Liberty* (Oxford: Oxford University Press, 1969), pp. xlvi, lxi.

7 This identification, together with its "right" counterpart, derives first from the historical positioning of the members of the Third Estate, as opposed to the nobility, in the French Etats-Généraux in 1789, to the left and right, respectively, of the king—one of those oddly influential historical accidents that pervade modern languages. It should also be noted that, at least in the former Soviet Union and no doubt elsewhere as well, a complete switch in the old convention has been observed on occasion, with Nozickeans being identified as the radicals, hence "leftists."

8 This example of a supposedly illegitimate use of the word *liberty* (negative *or* positive) was employed by Berlin himself with respect to African and Asian nationalist movements in *Two Concepts of Liberty*, p. 43. His views on this point have proved particularly controversial. See my " 'Two Concepts of Liberty' Thirty Years Later: A Sartre-Inspired Critique," *Social Theory and Practice 16*, 3 (Fall 1990): 313–316.

9 An excellent treatment of Marx's thought from this perspective is the book by George Brenkert, *Marx's Ethics of Freedom* (London and Boston: Routledge Kegan Paul, 1983).

10 I have discussed this point in a response to Steven Lukes, "Rights and the Marxian Tradition," *Praxis International 4*,1 (April 1987): pp. 57–74.

11 Carol Gould, *Rethinking Democracy: Freedom and Social Cooperation in Politics, Economy, and Society* (Cambridge: Cambridge University Press, 1988), Chap. 7, pp. 190–214.

12 See "Visions from the Ashes: The Philosophical Life in Bulgaria, 1945–1992," by Ivanka Raynova, co-authored by this writer, in *Philosophy and Political Change in Eastern Europe*, special issue of *The Monist*, forthcoming.

Chapter Six

1 John Rawls, *A Theory of Justice* (Cambridge, Mass.: Harvard University Press, 1971), p. 3. Rawls is clearly referring primarily to substantive, as distinguished

from procedural, justice. The latter is a leading topic in the philosophy of law, and it has also arisen implicitly in our discussion of rights.

[2] I put the word "facts" in quotation marks because I have the greatest reservations about Rawls' blithe assumption that these two disciplines are based on universal and indubitable facts in the sense intended. See pp. 994–995 of my early review of *A Theory of Justice*, "Social Theory *Sub Specie Aeternitatis:* A New Perspective," *Yale Law Journal 81*, 5 (April 1972).

[3] *A Theory of Justice*, p. 302.

[4] Ibid, p. 542.

[5] Among the best-known are Allen Wood, "The Marxian Critique of Justice," *Philosophy and Public Affairs 1*, 3 (Spring 1972): 224–282, and Robert Tucker, *The Marxian Revolutionary Idea* (New York: Norton, 1969), Chap. 3, pp. 37–53, reprinted *Nomos* VI: *Justice* (1963). See my reply, "The Concept of Justice in Marx, Engels, and Others" in *Ethics 85*, 3 (April 1975): 204–218.

[6] Thomas Wartenberg, *The Forms of Power* (Philadelphia: Temple University Press, 1990).

[7] Eléanor H. Kuykendall, "Toward an Ethic of Nurturance: Luce Irigaray on Mothering and Power," in Joyce Trebilcot, ed., *Mothering: Essays in Feminist Theory* (Totowa, N.J.: Rowman and Allenheld, 1984), p. 264.

[8] To get some sense of this approach, see the anthology, *Critical Legal Studies*, ed. Allan C. Hutchinson (Totowa, N.J.: Rowman & Littlefield, 1989), especially the essays by Clare Dalton and Mark Kelman, pp. 195–225.

[9] A good representative of this movement is Drucilla Cornell, *Beyond Accommodation* (New York and London: Routledge, 1991). Her critique of Robin West's "essentialism" in this book illustrates the presence of significant disagreement among feminist legal theorists over just how to characterize male/female differences for the purpose of analyzing injustices of the type in question.

[10] One example is the essay by Nancy Fraser, "Women, Welfare, and the Politics of Need Interpretation," pp. 144–160 in her *Unruly Practices* (Minneapolis: University of Minnesota Press, 1989).

[11] Jean-Francois Lyotard, *The Differend: Phrases in Dispute*, tr. G. Van Den Abbeele (Minneapolis: University of Minnesota Press, 1988), p. xi. See also Lyotard and Jean-Loup Thébaud, *Just Gaming*, tr. W. Godzich (Minneapolis: University of Minnesota Press, 1985).

[12] Iris Marion Young, *Justice and the Politics of Difference* (Princeton, N.J.: Princeton University Press, 1990).

Chapter Seven

[1] This is the focus of the final chapter of a too-much-neglected book by A. P. d'Entrèves, *The Notion of the State: An Introduction to Political Theory* (Oxford: Clarendon Press, 1967), pp. 222–230.

2 Rawls, op. cit., p. 283. (Note, however, that in the final, less widely cited part of his book, which deals with questions of goodness under the title, "Ends," Rawls does acknowledge the importance of the concept of *community* and strongly rejects [p. 521] the ideal of a "private society" in which individuals are concerned exclusively with their own private ends.)

3 See Gilligan's *In a Different Voice: Psychological Theory and Women's Development* (Cambridge, Mass.: Harvard University Press, 1982).

4 When it is referenced at all in most current dictionaries, communitarianism tends to be defined as a form of communism rather than as a broad movement in contemporary social philosophy.

5 Alisdair MacIntyre, *After Virtue* (South Bend, Ind.: University of Notre Dame Press, 1981).

6 Alisdair MacIntyre, *Whose Justice? Which Rationality?* (South Bend, Ind.: University of Notre Dame Press, 1988).

7 Will Kymlicka, *Liberalism, Community and Culture* (Oxford: Clarendon Press; New York: Oxford University Press, 1989).

8 Eugene Zamiatin, *We*, tr. G. Zilboorg (New York: Dutton, 1952).

9 George Orwell, *1984* (Oxford: Clarendon Press, 1984).

10 Aldous Huxley, *Brave New World* (New York: Harper, 1946).

11 Margaret Atwood, *The Handmaid's Tale* (New York: Fawcett Crest, 1985).

12 This is the thrust of the classic defense of the utopian element in Marx's theory; see Ernst Bloch's *The Principle of Hope*, tr. N. Plaice, S. Plaice, and P. Knight (Cambridge, Mass.: MIT Press, 1986).

13 Jean-Paul Sartre, *Critique de la raison dialectique*, II (Paris: Gallimard, 1985).

14 See, for example, Mihailo Marković, *From Affluence to Praxis: Philosophy and Social Criticism* (Ann Arbor: University of Michigan Press, 1974).

15 Frank Cunningham, *Democratic Theory and Socialism* (Cambridge: Cambridge University Press, 1987).

16 Op. cit.

17 Ernesto Laclau and Chantal Mouffe, *Hegemony and Socialist Strategy: Towards a Radical Democratic Politics* (London: Verso, 1985).

18 Peter Kropotkin, *Mutual Aid: A Factor in Evolution* (New York: New York University Press, 1972).

19 Leonard Harris, "Justice and the Concept of Racism," in A. Zegeye, L. Harris, and J. Maxted, eds., *Exploitation and Exclusion: Race and Class in Contemporary U.S. Society* (London: Hans Zell, 1991), pp. 28–44.

Chapter Eight

1 "In our choice, we are obviously guided by ethical and political preferences. A person whose political attitude is one of nationalism and imperialism will naturally be inclined to accept the hypothesis of the primacy of national law. A person whose

sympathies are for internationalism and pacifism will be inclined to accept the hypothesis of the primacy of international law." Kelsen, *General Theory of Law and State*, tr. A. Wedberg (New York: Russell & Russell, 1961), p. 388.

[2] L. Jonathan Cohen, *The Principles of World Citizenship* (Oxford: Blackwell, 1954).

[3] Wilfrid Desan, *The Planetary Man*, Vols. I and II (New York: Macmillan, 1972); Vol. III, *Let the Future Come* (Washington, D.C.: Georgetown University Press, 1987).

[4] Isaiah Berlin, *Two Concepts of Liberty* (Oxford: Clarendon Press, 1958), p. 43.

[5] Michael Walzer, *Just and Unjust Wars: A Moral Argument with Historical Illustrations* (New York: Basic Books, 1977).

[6] Christopher Stone, *Should Trees Have Standing? Toward Legal Rights for Natural Objects* (Los Angeles: W. Kaufmann, 1974).

[7] Marx, *Capital* (Moscow: Foreign Languages Publishing House, 1962), Vol. III, p. 757.

BIBLIOGRAPHY

Adorno, T. W., and Else Frenkel-Brunswik. *The Authoritarian Personality* (abridged). New York: Norton, 1983.

Alighieri, Dante. *Monarchy and Three Political Letters*, tr. D. Nicholl and C. Hardie. Westport, Conn.: Hyperion, 1989.

Aquinas, Thomas. *Selected Political Writings*, ed. A. P. d'Entreves, tr. J. G. Dawson. New York: Macmillan, 1959.

Arendt, Hannah. *The Human Condition*. Chicago: University of Chicago Press, 1970.

Aristotle. *The Nicomachean Ethics*, tr. T. Irwin. Indianapolis: Hackett, 1985.

_____. *Politics*, tr. E. Barker. Oxford: Oxford University Press, 1946.

Augustine, Saint. *The City of God*. Garden City, N.Y.: Image Books, 1958.

Beauvoir, Simone de. *The Second Sex*, tr. H. M. Parshley. New York: Random House, 1989.

Beccaria, Cesare. *On Crimes and Punishments*, tr. H. Paolucci. New York: Macmillan, 1963.

Berlin, Isaiah. *Four Essays on Liberty*. Oxford: Oxford University Press, 1969.

Bloch, Ernst. *The Principle of Hope*, 3 vols., tr. Neville Plaice, et al. Cambridge, Mass.; MIT Press, 1986.

Bosanquet, Bernard. *The Philosophical Theory of the State*. Charlottesville, Va.: Ibis, 1986.

Boxill, Bernard. *Blacks and Social Justice*. Totowa, N.J.: Rowman and Allanheld, 1984.

Brenkert, George. *Marx's Ethics of Freedom*. Boston: Routledge & Kegan Paul, 1983.

Burke, Edmund. *Reflections on the Revolution in France*, ed. J. G. Pocock. Indianapolis, Ind.: Hackett, 1987.

Cicero. *On the Commonwealth (De Re Republica)*, tr. G. H. Sabine and S. B. Smith. New York: Macmillan, 1929.

Cornell, Drucilla. *Beyond Accommodation: Ethical Feminism, Deconstruction, and the Law*. New York: Routledge, 1991.

————, et al., eds. *Deconstruction and the Possibility of Justice*. New York: Routledge, 1992.

Cunningham, Frank. *Democratic Theory and Socialism*. Cambridge: Cambridge University Press, 1987.

Dewey, John. *The Public and Its Problems*. Athens: Ohio University Press, 1954.

Dussel, Enrique. *Philosophy of Liberation*, tr. Martinez, Aquila, and C. Morkovsky. Maryknoll, N.Y.: Orbis Books, 1985.

Dworkin, Ronald, *Taking Rights Seriously*. Cambridge, Mass.; Harvard University Press, 1977.

Engels, Friedrich. *Ludwig Feuerbach and the Outcome of Classical German Philosophy*. New York: International Publishers, 1988.

————. *Origin of the Family, Private Property, and the State*, ed. E. B. Leacock. New York: International Publishers, 1972.

————. *Socialism: Utopian and Scientific*. New York: International Publishers, 1935.

Entrèves, Alessandro Passerin d'. *Natural Law: An Introduction to Legal Philosophy*. London: Hutchinson University Library, 1970.

————. *The Notion of the State: An Introduction to Political Theory*. Oxford: Oxford University Press, 1967.

Foucault, Michel. *Discipline and Punish: The Birth of the Prison*, tr. A. Sheridan. New York: Random House, 1979.

Fraser, Nancy. *Unruly Practices: Power, Discourse, and Gender in Contemporary Social Theory*. Minneapolis: University of Minnesota Press, 1989.

Gould, Carol. *Rethinking Democracy: Freedom and Social Cooperation in Politics, Economy, and Society*. Cambridge: Cambridge University Press, 1989.

Gramsci, Antonio. *Prison Notebooks: Selections*, tr. Q. Hoare and G. N. Smith. New York: International Publishers, 1971.

Habermas, Jürgen. *Legitimation Crisis*, tr. T. McCarthy. Boston: Beacon, 1973.

————. *The Theory of Communicative Action*, 2 vols., tr. T. McCarthy. Boston: Beacon Press, 1985 (Vol. I) and 1989 (Vol. II).

Hart, Herbert L. A. *The Concept of Law*. Oxford: Clarendon Press, 1961.

Hayek, Friedrich. *The Road to Serfdom*. Chicago: University of Chicago Press, 1944.

Hegel, George W. F. *Lectures in the Philosophy of History*, tr. J. Sibree. New York: Dover, 1956.

————. *The Phenomonology of Spirit*, tr. A. V. Miller and J. N. Findlay. Oxford: Oxford University Press, 1977.

————. *The Philosophy of Right*, tr. T. M. Knox. Oxford: Oxford University Press, 1942.

Hobbes, Thomas. *Leviathan*, ed. C. B. Macpherson. New York: Viking, 1982.

Hume, David. *Moral and Political Philosophy*, ed. H. D. Aiken. New York: Hafner, 1970.

Hutchinson, Allan C., ed. *Critical Legal Studies*. Totowa, N.J.: Rowman & Littlefield, 1987.

Jaggar, Alison. *Feminist Politics and Human Nature*. Totowa, N.J.: Rowman & Allanheld, 1983.

Kant, Immanuel. *The Metaphysical Elements of Justice: Part I of the Metaphysics of Morals*. Indianapolis: Bobbs-Merrill, 1965.

————. *Perpetual Peace and Other Essays on Politics, History, and Moral Practice*, ed. and tr. T. Humphrey. Indianapolis: Hackett, 1983.

Kelsen, Hans. *General Theory of Law and State*. New York: Russell and Russell, 1961.

Kropotkin, Peter. *Mutual Aid*. Boston: Porter and Sargent, 1976.

Kymlicka, Will. *Liberalism, Community, and Culture*. Oxford: Oxford University Press, 1991.

Laclau, Ernesto, and Chantal Mouffe. *Hegemony and Socialist Strategy: Towards a Radical Democratic Politics*. New York: Routledge, Chapman and Hall, 1985.

Lenin, V. I. *Essential Works of Lenin: 'What Is To Be Done?' and Other Writings*, ed. H. Christman. New York: Dover, 1987.

Locke, John. *A Letter Concerning Toleration*. Indianapolis: Hackett, 1983.

————. *Two Treatises of Government*, ed. P. Laslett. New York: Cambridge University Press, 1988.

Lukács, George. *History and Class Consciousness*, tr. R. Livingstone. Cambridge, Mass.: MIT Press, 1971.

Luxemburg, Rosa. *The Russian Revolution, and Leninism or Marxism?* Ann Arbor: University of Michigan Press, 1961.

Lyotard, Jean-François. *The Differend: Phrases in Dispute*, tr. G. Van Den Abbeele. Minneapolis: University of Minnesota Press, 1988.

Machiavelli, Niccolò. *The Prince and Other Discourses*, tr. L. Ricci. New York: McGraw-Hill, 1950.

MacIntyre, Alasdair. *After Virtue: A Study in Moral Theory*. Notre Dame, Ind.: University of Notre Dame Press, 1984.

————. *Whose Justice? Which Rationality?* Notre Dame, Ind.: University of Notre Dame Press, 1989.

Macpherson, C. B. *Democratic Theory: Essays in Retrieval*. New York: Oxford University Press, 1973.

Marcuse, Herbert. *One Dimensional Man*. Boston: Beacon, 1966.

————. *Reason and Revolution: Hegel and the Rise of Social Theory*. Atlantic Highlands, N.J.: Humanities Press, 1974.

Marković, Mihailo. *From Affluence to Praxis: Philosophy and Social Criticism*. Ann Arbor: University of Michigan Press, 1974.

Marx, Karl. *Capital: A Critique of Political Economy*, Vol. I, tr. B. Fowkes. New York: Random House, 1977.

————. *Critique of the Gotha Program*. New York: International Publishers, 1938.

————. *Early Writings*, tr. R. Livingstone and G. Benton. New York: Viking, 1992.

————, and Friedrich Engels. *The Communist Manifesto*. New York: International Publishers, 1970.

————, and Friedrich Engels. *The German Ideology*, Part I and selections from Parts II and III, ed. C. J. Arthur. New York: International Publishers, 1970.

McBride, William L. *The Philosophy of Marx*. London: Hutchinson, 1977.

————. *Sartre's Political Theory*. Bloomington: Indiana University Press, 1991.

————. *Social Theory at a Crossroads*. Pittsburgh: Duquesne University Press, 1980.

Mill, John Stuart. *Autobiography*, ed. J. H. Robson. New York: Viking, 1990.

————. *The Subjection of Women*, ed. S. M. Okin. Indianapolis: Hackett, 1988.

————. *Utilitarianism, On Liberty, Considerations on Representative Government*. New York: C. E. Tuttle, 1972.

Montesquieu, Baron de. *The Spirit of the Laws*. Glencoe, Ill.: The Free Press, 1969.

More, Thomas. *Utopia*. New York: C. E. Tuttle, 1991.

Nietzsche, Friedrich. *Beyond Good and Evil*, tr. R. J. Hollingdale. New York: Viking, 1990.

_____. *Thus Spoke Zarathustra*, tr. W. Kaufman. New York: Viking, 1978.

Nozick, Robert. *Anarchy, State and Utopia*. New York: Basic Books, 1977.

O'Neill, Onora. *The Faces of Hunger*. New York: Unwin Hyman, 1986.

Pateman, Carole. *Participation and Democratic Theory*. Cambridge: Cambridge University Press, 1976.

_____. *The Sexual Contract*. Stanford, Calif.: Stanford University Press, 1988.

Plato. *Apology of Socrates and Crito*, ed. A. S. Ash, tr. B. Jowett. Santa Barbara, Calif.: Bandanna Books, 1990.

_____. *The Laws of Plato*, tr. T. Pangle. Chicago: University of Chicago Press, 1988.

_____. *Republic*, tr. H. D. Lee. New York: Viking, 1955.

_____. *Statesman*, ed. M. Ostwald, tr. B. J. Skemp. New York: Macmillan, 1957.

Rawls, John. *A Theory of Justice*. Cambridge, Mass.; Harvard University Press, 1971.

Rousseau, Jean-Jacques. *Emile*, tr. and intro. A. Bloom. New York: Basic Books, 1979.

_____. *The Social Contract and the Discourses*, ed. J. H. Brumfitt and J. C. Hall, tr. G. D. Cole. New York: C. E. Tuttle, 1991.

Sandel, Michael. *Liberalism and the Limits of Justice*. New York: Cambridge University Press, 1982.

Sartre, Jean-Paul. *Critique of Dialectical Reason*: Vol. I, *Theory of Practical Ensembles*, ed. J. Rees, tr. A. Sheridan. New York: Routledge, Chapman and Hall, 1984.

_____. *Critique of Dialectical Reason*: Vol. II, tr. Q. Hoare. New York: Routledge, Chapman and Hall, 1991.

_____. *Search for Method*, tr. H. Barnes. New York: Random House, 1968.

Shklar, Judith. *The Faces of Injustice*. New Haven, Conn.: Yale University Press, 1990.

Smith, Adam. *The Wealth of Nations*. New York: McGraw-Hill, 1985.

Strauss, Leo. *What Is Political Philosophy? And Other Studies*. Chicago: University of Chicago Press, 1990.

Taylor, Charles. *Sources of the Self: The Making of the Modern Identity.* Cambridge, Mass.: Harvard University Press, 1989.

Thoreau, Henry David. *Walden and Civil Disobedience.* New York: Harper Collins, 1992.

Thucydides. *The Peloponnesian War,* tr. R. Crawley. New York: Random House, 1981.

Tocqueville, Alexis de. *Democracy in America,* 2 vols. New York: Random House, 1954.

Walzer, Michael. *Just and Unjust Wars.* New York: Basic Books, 1979.

————. *Spheres of Justice: A Defense of Pluralism and Equality.* New York: Basic Books, 1984.

Wartenberg, Thomas. *The Forms of Power: From Domination to Transformation.* Philadelphia: Temple University Press, 1990.

Weber, Max. *The Protestant Ethic and the Spirit of Capitalism.* New York: Macmillan, 1980.

Weldon, T. D. *The Vocabulary of Politics.* Harmondsworth, Sussex: Penguin, 1953.

Wolff, Robert P. *In Defense of Anarchism.* New York: Harper Collins, 1970.

Wollstonecraft, Mary. *A Vindication of the Rights of Woman,* ed. C. H. Poston. New York: Norton, 1975.

Young, Iris. *Justice and the Politics of Difference.* Princeton, N.J.: Princeton University Press, 1990.

Zegeye, A., L. Harris, and J. Maxted. *Exploitation and Exclusion: Race and Class in Contemporary U.S. Society.* London: Hans Zell, 1991.

INDEX